Roborovski Ham

Roborovski Hamsters

Roborovski Hamster book for care, feeding, handling, health and common myths.

by

Jonathan Durham

Table of Contents

Introduction

The word Hamster is derived from the German word 'Hamstern' which means 'to hoard' which is very apt as hamsters are well known for carrying – or hoarding – their food in their cheek pouches.

These incredibly cute rodents are found in the wild in a number of areas in the world and there are thought to be over twenty breeds of hamsters although only five species have been domesticated.

In the wild they spend a large portion of their lives in tunnels as this enables them to avoid predators and also keeps them safe from extreme temperatures. Their short strong legs and compact bodies are perfect for a life underground.

This book focuses on the Roborovski Hamster.

Chapter 1: The Roborovski Hamster

The Roborovski Hamster, also known as the Roborovski Dwarf Hamster or Robo, originates from the desert areas of Western and Eastern Mongolia, China and Russia. In the wild they dig and live in burrows with steep tunnels that can be as deep as six feet under the ground. While many people believe these animals are nocturnal they are actually crepuscular meaning they are most active at the twilight periods of dawn and dusk (early morning and early evening).

Their natural habitats are deserts and semi-deserts with little vegetation and as such they appear to need less water than other dwarf hamsters.

As a pet the Roborovski Hamster is relatively new having only been domesticated during the Nineteen Seventies although they are becoming increasingly popular.

With their short tail and beady black eyes these tiny little critters are adorable. Their long hind legs enable them to move at lightning fast speeds.

Unlike other species of hamsters the Roborovski only has one coat type with regards to texture and length. However there are two different colours you can buy. The first is the Agouti Roborovski Hamsters who have a sandy brown/beige coloured back speckled with black and a white belly and little white patches above their eyes which some people refer to as their 'eyebrows'.

The second colour is the White Face Roborovski Hamster, also referred to as a 'husky' is similar to the Agouti but, as the name suggests, its entire face is white.

It may be possible to find other colours but these are very rare and usually only found with breeders. These include the Platinum Roborovski Hamster which looks like a White Face but lighter in colour; as they become older their fur often turns a pure white.

Other types include the Red-Eyed, Mottled, Pied or Pure White Roborovski. I wouldn't recommend seeking out any type of 'special' Roborovski and would stick to the Agouti not only because they are easier to source and a 'designer hamster' would cost more in both time and money but also because to get the different colours they are usually inbred quite a lot which can cause health problems further down the bloodline which means you can never really be sure if you are getting a healthy pet.

Size

The Roborovski Hamster is the smallest of the dwarf hamsters. At birth they will be less than 2 centimetres (0.8 inches) long. Usually by two months of age they will have reached maturity and be fully grown, the maximum size for these hamsters is 4-5 centimetres (1.5-2 inches).

Life Span

Roborovski Hamsters have a fairly long life span when compared to the other species of hamsters that are kept as pets and can live to around three years although some have been known to reach four years or more.

Special Features

Whilst there are differences between the various hamster breeds there are some features that all hamsters, including the Roborovski, have in common.

Teeth

Hamsters are part of the rodent family which means they have the long front teeth called incisors that all rodents have. These teeth continually grow throughout their life which means you should give your Roborovski Hamster gnawing blocks or other toys for them to chew in order to wear these incisors down and keep them healthy. The good news is hamsters love to gnaw so as long as you provide them with suitable items on which to chew they should naturally keep those teeth at the right length. You should check your hamster's teeth at least once a week as if there are any problems you will need to consult a vet.

Feet And Claws

Compared to other species of dwarf hamsters, a Roborovski Hamster's feet and legs are larger than usual and this could be why they are so fast. They have four toes on their front paws and five toes on their back ones. Usually their claws will wear down naturally with all the running about they do but, just like with their teeth, these will need to be checked on a regular basis to make sure they're not damaged or overgrown.

You may see your Roborovski hamster standing on its back legs whilst using its front paws to hold food whilst they nibble on it which is super cute!

Cheek Pouches

This is what hamsters are known for – their adorable fat cheeks. Many people believe that hamsters just hold their food inside their mouths which pushes their cheeks out but this isn't true. They actually have pouches in their cheeks, separate to their mouths, which are made up of extra folds of skin enabling them to store their food until they wish to eat it. The hamster's face will bulge out when these pouches are full.

In the wild this adaptation means that they can forage over longer distances, storing the food that they find in their pouches until they return to their underground homes and can eat without fear of predators. Of course this isn't something that your hamster need worry about in captivity but it is a natural instinct so you will still find that your hamster will use its cheek pouches to store food, possibly carrying it from the feeding area to another part of the enclosure where it will eat it.

Cheek pouches have a very delicate lining so it is important to not put anything in your hamster's habitat that could damage this sensitive area such as straw.

Eyes

Despite their eyes being bright and alert a hamster's eyesight is actually very poor as they are both near sighted and colour blind. At birth they are blind and in adulthood can only see a few inches past their noses. In bright light they can barely see at all. It is thought that their poor eyesight is probably due to the fact that they spend most of their lives underground in the wild, only coming out at night, neither of which requires good eyesight.

Instead they will rely heavily on their other senses such as their excellent hearing and very acute sense of smell.

It is important that you don't startle your hamster as due to their poor eyesight they won't always recognise objects and sudden movements can frighten them. Always be slow and gentle especially when handling your hamster.

As they can't see very far your hamster won't have much sense of height which is why many people don't recommend housing them in cages that have multiple levels as they can fall easily. When handling ensure you are sitting on the floor rather than standing up and never allow your hamster to perch on your shoulder because they can quite easily jump out of your hand. Roborovski Hamsters are so quick they can soon leap away and a high fall is likely to result in broken limbs, damage to internal organs and even death.

Whiskers

These are an eyesight aid. Just like a cat, hamsters will use their whiskers to detect objects and low frequency movement. They can vibrate up to thirty times per second in short bursts also known as 'whisking' and this action sends information to the hamster about objects that are near to them that they may be unable to see. Please do not cut your hamster's whiskers; you may see posts on the internet that state they will grow back but cutting them can cause your hamster to injure themselves. These whiskers are long so that your hamster can detect the width of tunnels therefore they need to be at least as long as the widest part of your hamster otherwise they can get stuck in objects simply because they cannot see how small they are.

Scent Gland

Also known as flank glands or hip spots these can be a cause of confusion for new owners who don't know they exist and many show up at the vet's thinking they are a tumour. Roborovski Hamsters have a single scent gland on their undersides, slightly below their mid-section. They can stick out, sometimes can be hairless and often look greasy. They tend to be more prominent in males than females and it is thought that they are used for marking their territory and to signal when they're ready for mating, again possibly because they rely on their sense of smell rather than their eyesight. They become more obvious at maturity both by sight and smell and the often powerful odour can be off putting. Be aware of these glands when handling because the smell can be transferred onto your hands so always wash with soap and water immediately after handling.

Male hamsters have been known to bite each other's scent glands so keep an eye out for any fighting should you have more than one male in the same cage. Separate them immediately should either hamster have any open wounds. Whilst Roborovski Hamsters can be housed together it is always better to keep them in their own enclosures if possible.

Male Or Female?

How To Identify
It can be difficult to identify whether your Roborovski Hamster is a male or a female; if you are just keeping one as a single pet it doesn't really matter but if you are keeping more than one and want to avoid unwanted pregnancies or if you wish to breed your hamsters then of course it becomes more important to know which one you have.

Usually with animals, size is often an indicator of sex unfortunately with the Roborovski Hamster because they are so tiny this isn't reliable. Some hamsters of this breed will stay tiny whilst others will grow slightly bigger regardless of whether they are male and female.

The best way to identify whether your hamster is a girl or a boy is to hold it firmly by the 'scruff' which is the skin at the back of its neck but be careful not to trap your hamster's ears. If held properly in this way your hamster will not struggle and you will not hurt them.

For young hamsters around three and a half weeks or less it is easier because the female's eight teats will be visible however these soon become covered by fur and are less noticeable in adults unless the female is pregnant or nursing.

When trying to identify male and female adult Roborovski Hamsters, look at the two openings on their underside. On an adult male there is a very noticeable gap between the two but on a female there will be hardly any gap, usually just a slight 'line'.

Also look for the scent gland with older hamsters. The male scent gland is usually a bright yellowish stain in their middle. Females can have this visible scent gland but it is usually a lot fainter.

Sometimes the males' testicles are visible too, usually if they have been asleep and are warm and relaxed or if they have been paired up with a female for the first time or if they have been introduced to another male. Sometimes, like the females' teats, these won't be noticeable at all.

If you only have one adult Roborovski, identifying it's sex can be difficult if you don't have another one to compare it to. I would advise you look for photographs on the internet that are comparing male and females as this will help you decide which you have or join forums and post photographs of your own hamster and ask for advice.

Of course all hamsters are different and whilst some will very noticeably be male, others won't and even experienced breeders have been fooled leading them to sex their Roborovski Hamsters wrongly.

Which Should I Choose?
There's not really much difference between males and females in terms of temperament, care or life span requirements so other than personal preference it won't really make much difference whether your hamster is a boy or a girl. Just keep in mind that if you decide to keep a two or more in one cage and you don't have any intentions of breeding then they should all be the same sex to avoid unwanted babies and fighting.

Chapter 2: Before You Buy

Is A Roborovski Hamster For Me?

So you've decided to buy a hamster and are looking at the different breeds or maybe you've already fallen in love with one of these adorable little critters but want to know more about it before you bring it home. Before you rush out and buy one you may want to consider the following factors in order to decide if you (and your home) are suited to this type of hamster.

Firstly, as mentioned above, they are crepuscular creatures which means they are going to be asleep during the day. There are exceptions to this, for instance, on a cloudy or dreary dark day they may be tricked into thinking it's dawn or dusk and may be awake for a while but mostly they are going to be sleeping whilst you are awake. This may suit you as you are probably going to be out working during this time anyway but bear this in mind when you are looking for a suitable place to keep your hamster. I wouldn't recommend having one in your bedroom, for instance, because it will most likely keep you awake. I can tell you from personal experience that they are not quiet creatures and not everyone enjoys hearing them scrabbling around in their bedding or running around on a squeaky exercise wheel when they are trying to get to sleep!

Roborovski Hamsters, whilst small, take up a lot of space. They need to be kept indoors and as they are constantly on the go they require a cage that is big enough to give them exercise as well as hold toys such as a running wheel, tubes and so on to keep them entertained.

It is also important to keep them away from other animals. They are so timid even the slightest noise can send them running for cover so they ought to be kept in a room that is quiet as much as possible. If you have a noisy household with lots of other pets already then a Roborovski Hamster wouldn't make a good addition because they would be constantly stressed.

These creatures take up a lot of time. Feeding, cleaning the cage and monitoring their health are all tasks that need to be done regularly. It is better to do this in the evening when your hamster is awake otherwise you will disturb their sleep. If you are the type of person who likes to come in from work, have dinner and relax in front of the television rather than clean out a hamster cage then these probably aren't for you.

One final thing to take into consideration would be who will look after your Roborovski Hamster if you go away for the weekend or on holiday for a week or a fortnight? Unlike a dog or a cat you can't really put these creatures in a kennel and although nowadays there are some people who run 'pet hotels' for these type of small creatures unless you happen to have one nearby then you will need to organise somebody to come and look after your Roborovski Hamster. If you are lucky enough to have relatives, friends or a neighbour who could do this for you then great, if not you may have to reconsider whether to get a hamster or not because you can't just leave them alone for a few days without any care.

Do Roborovski Hamsters Make Good Pets?

One look at these cute little creatures and my heart melts and I want to shout 'yes these are great pets!' Of course this is a matter of opinion and whether you agree or not depends on what you are looking for in a pet.

If, for example, you are looking for one that you can pick up and cuddle or handle constantly then I would probably say that these are not great pets at all because these tiny little creatures rarely sit still and as such aren't going to be happy sat on your knee or in your hand for hours at a time. For this very reason a lot of people will describe them as a pet to watch rather than interact with and although they can be tamed they appear to tolerate handling rather than enjoy it and are much happier in their cage.

Having said that these creatures are adorable and are highly entertaining and even if you never pick them up you will get endless amusement from watching them charge around their cage and play with their toys. They each have their own personality and can be very sweet. Unlike some hamsters they rarely, if ever, nip and even when cornered they would prefer to run rather than bite and this is why I would describe them as wonderful pets.

Are Roborovski Hamsters Suited To Children?

A lot of people who want to buy a pet for their children often think of hamsters because they believe they are easy to look after, cute and can be handled easily. In my personal opinion the Roborovski Hamster is not suitable for any child because they are so fast it is really easy for a small child to panic and either drop these creatures or squeeze them too tight to stop them escaping.

Also they are such timid creatures children tend to be too noisy and unpredictable which can cause the hamsters a lot of stress.

Young children also don't always understand that the Roborovski Hamsters have a different routine and will want to pet them as soon as they come home from school or when they wake up in a morning which is usually when these creatures are asleep and shouldn't be disturbed.

Having said that if you have a child that is calm and happy to watch their hamster running about rather than wanting to play with them all the time then this type of animal may make a good pet for someone over the age of ten however I would always recommend that they are supervised by a responsible adult and that you help to clean and feed the hamster rather than allowing the child to do it by themselves.

Cost

Hamsters are generally cheap in comparison to other animals kept as pets but that doesn't mean there aren't costs to take into consideration. It is unrealistic to expect a child to pay for everything a hamster would need out of their pocket money, for example, and if you are buying one as a pet for a child you would need to make sure an adult would be able to supplement and help out when necessary, especially if any unexpected vet bills arose.

There main costs are listed below and are a mixture of both one off and recurring costs:

One-Off Costs
Roborovski Hamster - £5 - £15 (approximately $6 $20) depending on age and place purchased

Cage £30 - £110 (approximately $40-$147) depending on type and size.

Water bottle - £2 ($2.68) upwards depending on the type

Food dish - £5 ($6.69) upwards

Exercise Ball - £3.99 ($5.34)

Exercise wheel - £12.99 ($17.39)

Sand Bath £7 ($9.37) upwards

Sleeping House - £8 ($10.71) upwards

Travel cage - £6 (approximately $8)

Recurring Costs

Bedding - £2-£4 (approximately $2-$5) per month depending on cage size and type used

Food and Treats – approximately £5 ($6.69) a month depending on amount given

Chews - £1.89 ($2.53)

Toys

Seesaw - £1.79 ($2.40)

Climbing frame - £3.39 ($4.54)

Logs - £7 ($9.37)

Swing - £1.99 ($2.66)

Ladder £2.99 ($4)

Bridge £2.99 ($4) upwards

Flying Saucer - £5.65 ($7.56)

Chew Toys – £1.99 – £4.38 (approximately $2 - $5)

Other Costs

Vet Bills - £50 - £80 (approximately $60-$110) depending on area and reason for going

Please note prices were correct at the time of going to press - although these can change according to currency fluctuations which, of course is out of the author's control.

Okay so let's say that I buy a hamster for £10 – these prices may vary depending on where you live, the type of retailer you use and the age of the hamster, for example, I could probably buy a hamster from an animal shelter for a £5 donation/administration fee or I could spend £15 from a high end breeder if I want a Roborovski with an award winning family background. For the purpose of this example, I've just split the difference and will pretend I've purchased a baby hamster from a breeder for £10.

Next I want a cage – again you can buy small, wire bar cages for around £30 but if you want a larger, higher quality one then you will need to spend more. For this example we'll pretend that I've spent £90 on a glass aquarium style cage. Inside I will need a water bottle, again for one that hooks onto the side of a cage you can buy for around £2 but for ones that need to have a stand or fix to a glass cage you could be looking at £6 or more which is the figure I'll use in this example.

Right, so far I've spent £90 on an aquarium, £6 on a water bottle and £5 for a ceramic food dish. (Again prices may differ depending on quality and size but rather than use the cheaper prices I'm going to go for middle of the range ones. I would always recommend you pay more and get larger or higher quality items). If we add everything else that I've listed on the one off items list using the prices above the total is £148.98. In the grand scheme of things compared to other pets you could buy that isn't too high a price although some people may think that spending nearly £150 on a creature that cost £10 is a bit extortionate so it's all a matter of perspective.

The recurring costs are monthly ones and aren't actually too high, £10.89 if we take the higher estimates and again these will vary depending on how much you feed your hamster, for example, if you give tiny amounts each day then a bag of food may last you longer than a month whereas if you feed higher amounts of food and have more wastage a bag of hamster feed may not last you as long. You may purchase a more expensive, higher quality feed than the one I've counted in here and treats may cost more or less depending on what you purchase and the prices in your area.

With regards to toys if you purchased everything on the list at the prices given it will cost you £30.18 which is probably the most expensive outlay after the cage. You wouldn't have to spend this in one go, you could just pick three or four toys off the list and then add to your collection once a month or so and over time your toy collection will probably far exceed the estimate here. There are also a variety of different toys so you may find others that aren't on this list. You may choose not to spend any money on toys and make your own in which case your hamster would cost you a lot less.

Whilst these are estimates what this section does illustrate is that a Roborovski Hamster isn't all that expensive. You may invest around £200 at the start but then your monthly costs are fairly minimal.

The only risk you take is if your end up having a large vet bill, again dependent on the area you live in and the reason why you need a vet, as well as the type of vet you use – for instance, a vet that specialises in small animals may be more expensive than a general vet – and whether you need medication will all contribute towards the cost. If you keep your pet healthy and the cage clean however you can reduce the need for a vet. (That's not to say your hamster will never need a vet check but just that a hamster that is in a really clean cage with plenty of space in a stress free environment, lots of toys to keep them occupied and healthy food is less likely to get sick as often as one that is kept in a dirty cage with limited toys and poor quality food.

Where To Buy

Roborovski Hamsters are more difficult to find than other dwarf hamsters or Syrian Hamsters however that doesn't mean they are impossible to source just that you may have to do some research or wait a while in order to find one near to where you live. There are different options that you can choose from, all of which have advantages and disadvantages. I won't recommend one over the other, after all there are good and bad pet shops just like there are good and bad breeders and good and bad owners.

Pet Shops

These are probably the easiest place to source a Roborovski Hamster and the advantage of buying them from a store is that you have someone you can return to for advice or hold accountable should you buy a sick hamster. Some pet shop staff are brilliant and will be knowledgeable about the creatures they are selling and will be willing to tell you about them and even let you hold them.

Whilst you should have a cage already prepared for your new pet, if by any chance you don't then another advantage of buying in a store is that you can buy all the supplies that you need such as bedding, food, toys and so on from at the same time.

If you choose this route then always make sure the outlet you are buying from meets all the welfare needs of the animals in their care and that information is readily available. Check the cages are all clean and males and females have been housed separately. If you are in any doubt then don't buy. (A rule you should stick to whenever buying an animal no matter where you source it from)

I would advise you to research the pet shop first if possible and see if there are a lot of people online complaining as this could signal that the pets are less than healthy although often it just depends upon whether you have a good store in your area or not and bear in mind that many people will only write a review if they have something bad to say. There are a lot of mixed reviews about some of the large chain stores with many people saying that they have bought a hamster that is sick or a female hamster that was already pregnant so it may be worth looking for an independent store who specialises in hamsters as the care may be better and the hamsters healthier if staff and owners are more knowledgeable.

Breeder

This can either be somebody who breeds Roborovski Hamsters to make money or a hobbyist who breeds them purely for the fun of it. Usually the latter is better because if they are raising and breeding hamsters as a hobby they are usually a member of the Hamster Club and genuinely love these animals. That's not to say that all other breeders are just in it for the money but some are so you should be careful about whom you are buying from; as with pet shops, always research the breeder first.

I would always recommend you visit the breeder and ask to see the full set up and the parents not just the hamster you are buying. By looking at the parents you can get an indication of the babies' sociability and temperament as well as ensuring that all the hamsters are well cared for. As above, always check the conditions of the cage and the animals themselves.

A responsible breeder will be enthusiastic and willing to discuss the hamsters with you, providing information such as what the babies have been eating, what their temperament is like, whether they have been handled and how they react to this and so on. Ideally they will provide you with a weeks' worth of food as sudden changes in diet can make these creatures very ill. At the very least they should tell you exactly what they have been eating, including food mixes so you can buy the same or similar.

If you find a breeder who is unwilling to let you meet at their house and/or refuses to let you see the parents and/or don't willingly give you the information you ask for then I would go elsewhere.

Adoption/Rescue Pet

Many people end up with baby hamsters either because they have unwittingly bought one that was already pregnant or because they have sexed their hamsters wrong and ended up with an unwanted litter. The result is that plenty of rescue centres have thousands of animals needing to be re-homed and it is wonderful to think that you can give a creature a second chance at life. Often they require only a small donation or an administration fee.

The downside of adopting a pet from a shelter is that they may be more skittish than normal and you may not know the whole truth about why they are in the rescue centre in the first place. It may simply be that the owners had accidentally bred their pets or had bought a hamster and then changed their mind or realised that they couldn't look after them but they may also have been neglected or mistreated which could make them more wary of humans and have a diverse effect on their temperament making them harder to tame. If you are not bothered about handling and are happy to have them as a pet to watch then adoption may be a good option for you.

Another consideration is that you may not really know how old the hamster is that you are adopting. As these creatures have short life spans anyway you may end up adopting one that only lives a year or two because it is already halfway through its life. Again, if your main concern is giving a hamster a happy life for as long as you can then adoption would be a great thing for you to do.

The last thing to think about is that if you have set your heart on a Roborovski Hamster it may be a while before one turns up in your local adoption centre. If you're happy to wait then that's great but if not you may want to consider another place to purchase. Never buy a hamster from a pet store then adopt a Roborovski Hamster from a shelter, expecting to be able to put them in the same cage as they will have a higher chance of being able to co-habit successfully if they have been raised together from babies.

Preloved
When I say 'preloved' or second-hand' I mean a hamster that somebody has bought and is then selling on themselves rather than sending them to a shelter.

I would always recommend that you visit the hamster in person and see them in their previous home so that you can get an idea of the environment they've lived in and how well cared for they have been. You can also talk to the owner in person and get an idea of why they are selling their hamster – talking to them face to face should give you a better idea about whether they are telling the truth or not.

Second hand Roborovski Hamsters can be bought cheap, usually around £5 ($6 or $7 in the US) or even £25 ($33) with the full set up of cage and toys (although you would need to check that the setup is suitable before purchasing as many people house these hamsters in a cage that is far too small).

The disadvantage of purchasing this way is, once again, you can't always be sure how old the hamster is that you are buying or why that person is selling it. I'm quite cynical and would be wary about trusting someone who is telling me that they are selling a hamster that is only four or five months old as I would worry about why they had only kept it for such a short time – is it sick or has it a bad temperament? Or are they lying and selling a hamster that is actually already halfway through its life? Some people are genuine however and there are many reasons for selling a hamster, possibly they have purchased it on whim without doing any research first and only realised afterwards how much care these animals need or possibly they have lifestyle changes that no longer accommodate the hamster. My advice is always quiz the seller thoroughly and if you are not happy about the answers they give you or are unsure about the health of the hamster then don't buy.

What To Look For

Whether adopting, buying a previously owned pet or a brand new one from a breeder or pet shop, you need to give it a health check before purchasing. The three key places to check for disease are the eyes, mouth and tail.

Listed below are all signs of an underlying medical condition; should you spot any of the following then please don't buy the hamster.

- Wet faeces/diarrhoea in the cage or stuck to the animal's bottom – some sellers such as pet shops and breeders will more than likely have several hamsters in one cage but if you spot this in the cage or on any of the animals then please don't buy any because it is a sign of a condition called Wet Tail which is highly infectious, if one hamster in the enclosure has it then the odds are they all will.

- Firm, warm, swollen stomach

- Sunken, dull looking eyes – a Roborovski Hamster's eyes should be alert and bright, there should be no tear staining or discharge.

- Drinking lots of water or not drinking at all – You may not see a Roborovski Hamster drink anything in the time you are visiting a seller as, being desert creatures they don't need a lot, but if you do see one gulping back lots of water then don't buy it as this could signal a medical problem.

- Discharge from nostrils – a hamster's nostrils should be clean and the creature should be breathing easily
- Persistent sneezing or coughing – whilst this could just be an allergy it may be a sign of something worse, just like humans hamsters can catch cold but for them they can be fatal.

- Sitting in a hunched up position – this could mean the hamster is unwell or in pain.

- Abnormal lumps and bumps on body – could be an injury or cancer or another medical problem

- Weakness, wobbliness or difficulty standing up, walking or using any of its limbs.

- Dirty coat – their coat should be clean and smooth without any tangling, matting or staining on fur. There should be no bald patches or thin fur.

- Not moving - whilst Roborovski Hamsters are more active during the early hours of the morning and evening if they are awake then they should be active whether this be running around, using the exercise wheel or playing with other toys, eating, burrowing or doing some sort of activity. These creatures very rarely sit still unless they are sleeping so make sure you see them awake wherever possible. If they are asleep and are picked up they should instantly wake up and start moving around at high speed.

- Persistent scratching.

- Injuries – check that their ears aren't torn or damaged and that there are no injuries to their paws and claws and no scars.

Whilst I have tried to include the main items to watch out for this list is by no means exhaustive and if you see anything at all that concerns you then don't buy. You will most likely become very attached to the Roborovski Hamster that you purchase and buying one that may already be sick will not only cause you a lot of stress and heartache but may also cost you a lot of money too. A responsible seller will always let you go home and think about it rather than giving you a hard sell. Don't be fooled by the "I have many interested customers and they could be sold out by the time you next return" line – yes, this may be a risk of going away to consider your purchase but you will always be able to find someone else selling these creatures at some point, it is far better to wait a few extra weeks or months if someone else does buy the hamster you were considering than to purchase one that is sick.

General Points To Remember

Wherever you buy from try and go early morning or early evening, for instance, if buying in from a pet shop or pet shelter go just before it closes so that the Roborovski Hamsters will be awake, if buying from breeder or a private owner ask if you can go after work or early evening.

If you can, try and be confident about how to sex a Roborovski Hamster before buying, this way you can try and identify for yourself whether the hamsters are male or female and this could help you avoid buying one that is already pregnant (although you would have to check all the hamsters in the cage to ensure there wasn't an accidental mix up).

Never choose a hamster just because it looks cute. All Roborovski Hamsters in my opinion are adorable but buying one that is curled up in a tiny ball because you think it may be easy to tame isn't the right way to choose. Go for one that is running about and active because they are more likely to be healthy.

Always ask to handle the hamsters before you buy and give it a quick health check. Never buy via the internet because you don't know that the animal you have seen in the photograph online is the one you are getting. Plus without seeing it in person you don't know if it is healthy. I would also worry about it being delivered and how comfortable or traumatic the journey would be.

Check the cage conditions thoroughly. Wherever you go the hamsters' cage should be clean and not overcrowded with males and females being housed separately.

You may be given a cardboard box in which to take your new pet home however I would recommend that you invest in a small carry case and put some bedding in. Not only will this give your hamster a comfier journey but also eliminates the risk of it chewing through a cardboard box on the way home. Whilst they are an extra expense they are good little temporary homes to place these pets in whilst you are cleaning out their actual cage and are handy should you ever need to take your hamster to the vet.

Pair or Separate?

This is a subject that has very mixed reviews with some people saying that Roborovski Hamsters are very sociable and enjoy living in a pair or a small group of three or four whilst others say they should be separated because if a fight breaks out it can result in injury or death to one or more of the hamsters. Some will even go so far as to say that it will shorten the life span of all the creatures if they are housed together.

In my experience and from the extensive research I've done over the years Roborovski Hamsters are a bit like people in that they are all individual and have very different personalities, temperaments and preferences. Whilst some seem happy in a pair or a group, others are more content on their own.

Personally I would be wary about putting two hamsters together, regardless of species, just in case a fight broke out whilst I wasn't around. If you do want more than one hamster however then just be vigilant and split them up at any sign of trouble.

Only ever put two hamsters of the same breed together, for instance, you cannot house a Roborovski Hamster with another species of dwarf hamster.

Never buy two Roborovski Hamsters from different litters and expect them to live together. Although this can be successful - after all breeders have to source hamsters from different litters in order to breed - to cohabit for life successfully they have to be introduced at a very young age and it is always recommended that you buy two from the same litter in order to have a better chance of them getting along.

Unless you want to breed always check that all the hamsters you buy are the same sex, don't just take the seller's word for it as some hamsters can be mixed up, especially in pet shops.

I have heard many people moan that they have bought two Roborovski Hamsters with the intention of putting them in the same cage and therefore believe they only need one wheel, one food bowl, one sleeping house and a few toys between them. This assumption that the hamsters can share is not true. Even if you have one enclosure you will need a wheel for each hamster, numerous tunnels and toys, a sleeping house and food bowl each. Your hamster cage should be large enough that they can have space to themselves if they wish to do so. Don't be surprised if your hamsters suddenly start fighting despite having been together since they were babies, they can become more territorial as they get older and can take a dislike to one another in a matter of seconds so be prepared to buy another cage (and always have a travel cage handy that can make a temporary home for one so that you can separate immediately if a problem arises rather than leaving them together whilst you source a new cage.)

Many owners have stated that Roborovski Hamsters that live alone are much easier to tame than those that live together. Whether this is because they bond with their owners rather than their cage buddies or purely because they don't have another hamster to encourage them I'm not entirely sure but those kept in a group or a pair tend to run around their enclosure ridiculously fast whenever their owner appears, seemingly copying each other.

If you do keep more than one hamster to a cage then monitor regularly. It may not always be obvious that a hamster is being bullied. As well as open wounds, look out for a hamster walking around with constantly full cheek pouches or one that is thinner and smaller than the rest as these are signs that the hamster isn't being allowed to eat in peace or is being prevented from any food access at all. Stereotypical behaviour such as constantly running back and forth along the edges of the cage or running continual laps around and around the cage are also signs that the cage mates aren't quite as harmonious as you may think.

If you see any signs that one of more of your hamsters are stressed you should consider putting them in separate cages.

If you spot an open wound but the affected hamster doesn't seem all that bothered then they may just have been scratched or bitten whilst playing or it may be a one off argument. Consider adding more wheels, food and food dishes as well as extra tunnels and if this doesn't seem to help then separate the hamsters.

If you have more than two hamsters and decide you need to separate one then you can either remove the bully or the one who is being bullied. Whilst it may seem kinder to remove the one who seems to be the instigator of all the trouble this may not solve the problem because chances are another hamster within the group will replace them so the one who is being bullied may continue to be attacked. Generally the safest option is to remove the one who seems to be being picked on all the time, they may even be happier by themselves and you could always consider reintroducing them later as long as this is done correctly.

If you do decide to introduce two Roborovski Hamsters from different litters then you need to do this very carefully. Never put one hamster in the other one's cage as these animals are so territorial that this is almost guaranteed to cause a fight.

The best way to get the animals used to each other's scent without putting them together is to take some bedding out of each cage and swap it around

– so the first hamster has some bedding from the second hamster's cage and vice versa. Put the cages next to each other so they can get used to seeing one another without physically occupying the same space.

The next step is to put them somewhere that is neutral territory that neither of them have been before such as a large play box. Let the two of them sniff around and introduce themselves. Roborovski Hamsters will 'box' with each other and may make a lot of squeaking noises. This is normal behaviour and nothing to worry about but make sure you know what signs to look out for as their friendly playing can turn nasty very quickly.

Do this several times and if this is successful you can put them together. Use a brand new cage that neither hamster has been in before and make sure it is large and spacious. If you have had previous hamsters or pets in this cage then make sure you thoroughly disinfect it first so that there are no other animal smells remaining.

Ensure that there is a deep level of bedding, lots of nesting materials and put in two wheels, two food bowls, two water bottles, two sleeping houses and lots of toys. If you use litter boxes and sand baths there should be two of these as well. Make sure there is still plenty of space for them to run about, numerous tunnels and hiding places so that they can each have their own areas and be by themselves should they wish to do so.

If you see any of the signs mentioned above then separate and try re-introducing them again at a later date. The method for introducing should be exactly the same even if you the two hamsters have been in a cage together previously. Always make sure you let them meet on plenty of occasions on neutral ground before putting them in the same cage and always with plenty of supervision.

Chapter 3: Housing

Your hamster's cage is a critical aspect of their care, after all most of their lives will be spent here so it needs to be as perfect as possible in order to avoid injury and lengthen their life span.

Considerations

Generally hamster cages are either the glass aquarium types, made from a wire frame with solid base or made completely of plastic or Perspex. Mainly it is down to personal choice but when you are selecting a hamster cage it is important to consider the following factors:

Size

From your hamster's perspective this is the most important consideration. Roborovskis are known for how much ground they cover and experts state that the amount of distance these hamsters run each night is the equivalent of a human running 104.8 miles. With this much running the more floor space you can give them, the better. A lot of hamster cages on the market are far too small even though they will be labelled as suitable for dwarf hamsters. These creatures will run around constantly and a cage that is small will lead to boredom and compulsive behaviour issues such as chewing, pacing and circling.

Another advantage to having a large cage is that it will take longer for ammonia (from their urine) to build up which leads to a cleaner cage and a healthier hamster.

Also if you have two or more Roborovskis in one cage they are likely to get along better because they won't have to constantly defend their space and will be able to get away from each other and have time alone if they wish to do so. Remember for two or more you need double the items as well.

Ease Of Cleaning

Hamsters are generally clean creatures so their cage should be spot cleaned on a daily basis with a proper clean once a week (although larger cages can go a little bit longer bedding should still be changed weekly). Whilst it may be novelty at first, cleaning a hamster cage soon becomes a chore so choose a cage that is easy to clean otherwise you will just end up putting it off at the expense of your pet's health.

Security And Safety

Hamsters are adept at climbing and this makes them great escape artists. They will climb the wire bars of a cage or their toys both as exercise and in order to get out. Cage lids and doors need to be secure as hamsters are experts at opening doors or pushing lids that are not fastened properly. Clips can be used on doors and lids to provide extra security. When choosing a cage, select one that it is high enough to leave space between the top of their toys and the lid so that your hamster is unable to climb out.

If you are choosing a cage with multiple levels or tubes make sure they are not so high that there is a risk your hamster will fall a long distance.

Roborovski Hamsters are wilier than most because they are so small. Usually no taller than an adult's thumb they can squeeze between the bars of a wire cage so if this is the type you are choosing make sure that the bars are less than a centimetre (around a quarter of an inch) apart. Usually the cages made specifically for hamsters have gaps that are too wide for a Roborovski Hamster so you may have to look for one that is designed for mice however remember that the size is important and this is where you may struggle as cages for mice tend to be smaller than those made for hamsters.

Ventilation

Air quality and condensation can quickly become an issue in a hamster cage if it has lots of enclosed compartments. The best cages are those that allow the air to circulate around it as much as possible. Whilst ensuring your cage is open to fresh air and well ventilated it must also offer protection from drafts. For this reason many people won't recommend the cages that connect together by tubes because your Roborovski Hamster can (and most likely will) take it's bedding into a tube which could lead to poor air flow and cause ventilation issues.

Chewing

All hamsters will chew, it's a natural habit and is a way of keeping their teeth blunt however this urge to chew can affect cage suitability because they can (and will) chew through pretty much anything. In plastic cages make sure that there are no exposed ridges or edges that your hamster can start chewing otherwise it is likely to escape. Wire cages are advantageous because they can't usually chew through the smooth plastic tray but some hamsters can become obsessed with chewing the bars. From this respect a glass aquarium type space is ideal because the smooth sides' means there is absolutely nothing your hamster can chew through or damage their teeth on.

Type of Cages

Glass

These are rectangular and similar to an aquarium. There are two variations available on the market now which are either all glass with a wire or mesh screen cover that latches to the top or a deep glass base with a second storey made of wire sides and top.

Whichever of these styles you choose they should be around ten gallons in size (around 37.9 Litres) The minimum size in centimetres is 75 length x 30 width x 30 cm height (30x12x12 inches) although if you can buy bigger then do so.

The all glass style with a mesh lid is a popular choice for Roborovski Hamsters because they give a good, all round view. Their smooth sides make them secure as the hamster cannot climb or chew its way out. The glass bases can be deep enough that they encourage digging but the solid sides mean that their bedding doesn't spill out. As they are all on one level your hamster cannot fall from a great height and injure itself.

The downside to these cages is that they can be expensive. One that is the minimum size can be around £90 upwards. (Approximately $118)
A two storey with a deep glass base and an upper level with wire sides and top can cost around £160 (approximately $210) upwards. The bigger the cage the more it will cost.

The other disadvantages are that they can be heavy and awkward to handle which means you won't be able to move it around easily. I don't see this as a problem if you are choosing a spot in the room and leaving your hamster there for the rest of its life just ensure that it is somewhere quiet where the hamster won't be disturbed by other pets, loud noises and other people.

It is difficult to clip anything on to the sides of a glass tank such as a water bottle which could mean you will have to purchase a more expensive bottle and stand for the cage.

Also it is not easy to expand a glass cage because you can't really build extra structures that join together. This means you would have to buy the biggest cage you can afford when you purchase your hamster. However I don't see this as an issue as you could make a maze or play box outside of the hamster's enclosure that it can run about in when you're there to supervise.

Just remember that whilst they look big once you have toys inside the glass cages often don't have a lot of empty floor space for running about so make sure you measure the cage carefully and try to imagine what it will look like once the equipment is all inside.

Cleaning is both a blessing and a curse with these enclosures. Personally I think they're great an all glass cage on one level with a screen top just has to be emptied and washed down which I think is easy. However other people disagree and see it as a disadvantage because they cannot be dismantled which means you have to lean over the cage and reach inside in order to give it a thorough clean and as the large ones can be so heavy it has to be cleaned in situ. Again it is really just personal preference. I would recommend that if you do use this type of cage you sit it on a desk or a table that allows you to easily reach inside and clean or capture your hamster rather than having to bend your back too much in order to do anything in the cage.

Wire With Plastic Base

These are probably the type of cage you think about when you talk about hamster houses and consist of a plastic box with wire top and sides. (You can buy cages that are completely made of wire including the bottom rather than having the plastic base but these aren't suitable for any hamster because they can get their feet trapped)

They are a great choice in that they are easy to clean, have large doors which enables you to reach in and catch your hamster, allow you to easily watch your hamster's antics through the metal bars and they are lightweight, easy to move, have great ventilation and are relatively inexpensive. One of these style houses can cost you around £30 upwards (Approximately $40).

However the disadvantages are that they can be draughty, bedding can come through the wire sides when your hamster is digging like a maniac and they can easily become obsessed with chewing the wire. They can also climb the wire bars so there is a risk of them falling and hurting themselves.

Many people will say that these hamster cages are not suitable for Roborovskis for the reason mentioned above – that they can squeeze through the bars and it tends to be that the larger the cage, the bigger the gap between the bars is although you can buy mouse cages which tend to have less space between the bars but again you would have to choose these carefully and measure before you purchased.

Connectable Cage

These may be harder to imagine but they usually consist of a small 'starter home' which have plastic tubes and other boxes and things that link together. They are usually colourful and can look funky and fun.

The advantages of these are that they are different to a normal, plain hamster cage and you can have lots of tunnels which reflect their natural life in the wild and gives them plenty of places to run and explore stopping them from becoming bored. If you have more than one Roborovski then theoretically they can have so much space they will get along better because they can spend time alone should they wish to do so. You can buy a few bits at a time and expand as much as you want. The basic starter houses can start from around £38 (around $50) with the extra add-on tubes and so on priced from £5 ($6.55) depending on the size and style.

The disadvantages are that they can be ridiculously difficult to clean. You need to dismantle everything and clean it all separately which can take a long time.

If you have multiple levels then there is a risk of your hamster falling and injuring itself and Roborovski Hamsters can find it difficult to climb up vertical tunnels, especially those made of smooth plastic.

Ventilation and air flow is not as good in these type of cages and the air can quickly become stagnant and stale. Plastic can also heat up in the summer which can lead to suffocation.

If your Roborovski Hamster decides to hide in a tube it can be very difficult to catch and take out of the cage. Whilst this isn't a problem if you don't want to handle your pet often, you still need to be able to regularly check them for any signs of illness and wouldn't be very good if you needed to take them to a vet.

Each cage has its own advantages and disadvantages and therefore you should weigh these up before buying your hamster cage. The three types mentioned above are the most popular types but you can buy other variations on these so it is worth doing your research as you may find a different type that you prefer. The prices given above are for the minimum recommended size – you can buy cheaper cages which are smaller and of course, larger cages will be more expensive. (Also note the prices given were correct at the time of going to print and are subject to changes which are out of the author's control) I would always recommend spending more money and buying as big a cage as possible as this may save you money in the long run if you don't have to keep buying extra additions or a bigger enclosure in the future if you discover that your hamster isn't happy with the size.

Points to remember
Ventilation is an important consideration – make sure that if you have a glass enclosure that it has a secure wire screen cover that is latched to the top otherwise your hamster will be able to push the screen to get out. If you have plastic tubes that connect consider the airflow and always check your hamster regularly.

If your enclosure has smooth sides, don't be fooled into thinking that you don't need a lid – your hamster will find a way to reach the top usually this will be by climbing on its toys.

Don't put cages that have wire bars next to curtains or anything that the hamster can pull inside the cage – I have known Roborovski Hamsters that have squeezed through their cage bars and climbed the curtains!

Check that your hamster cage is safe with nothing sharp that the hamster can chew on.

When purchasing buy as big as possible. Consider the toys that you will be putting in for your hamster's entertainment *before* you buy it – you will be amazed at how much space a wheel and a few tubes takes up!

Remember Robo Hamsters are tiny and have difficulty climbing smooth tubes vertically so try to place them so that your hamster can run through them without there being a steep incline.

Check that your hamster can't fall from high distances.

Keep your cage out of draughts, direct sunlight and direct heat.

Clean your hamster cage regularly.

Give your hamster(s) separate areas for sleeping, toileting, playing, et cetera. This makes it easier for you as you can just change the substrate in the toilet area on a daily basis rather than the whole cage and keeps your hamster cleaner and healthier.

Make sure you provide lots of toys and activities so your hamster doesn't get bored.

Chapter 4: Bedding And Nesting

Some people distinguish between the two, others don't. For the sake of this book and to make it easier if you are researching elsewhere my definitions are bedding – or substrate as some people refer to it – is the material that covers the entire floor of the cage. Although it is recommended that a 7.5 centimetre (approximately 3 inch) layer is used, your hamster will always prefer a 15 centimetre (approximately 6 inch) layer if possible as they love to dig and tunnel. When choosing bedding material look for one that will absorb both odour and moisture (from urine and leaking water bottles) as not only will this be better for your pet but will also reduce your cleaning duties.

Your hamster won't just sleep anywhere and they will need a designated sleeping corner with a small house. The material you put inside this is what I will refer to as nesting material. This needs to be soft on their face and feet.

Generally the materials you use for bedding can be used for nesting but some people prefer to use different types so that the nesting material is softer whilst the bedding is easier to dig in. You will probably find that your hamster will move their material around their cage anyway, for instance, they may take their nesting material to a tube and make their own nest or they may take the bedding material into their sleeping house and use it to block the entrance to make them feel more secure. Whatever you choose make sure it is safe if your hamster ingests it and has no sharp edges that could cause injury.

There are many different options and which ones you choose can have an effect on your pet so it is important to select the right materials. It can be a matter of trial and error as all hamsters are different and some may have allergies to certain materials. Some Roborovski Hamsters like eating their bedding so you need to make sure that it is safe just in case they decide to have a nibble.

Yes, cost may be a factor but you should also consider your pet's health and happiness too so choose one that is comfy and makes them feel secure.

The main type of bedding and nesting materials available on the market at the moment are;

Wood Shavings/Chips

This is the most popular type to use as bedding as it can be fairly cheap and bought in bulk. They are great for your hamster to dig about in and are easy to find in pet stores. Keep your eye out for large splintery pieces when putting them into your hamster's cage as sometimes these aren't fully processed, especially the cheaper ones and these can hurt your hamster's feet or cheek pouches.

The downside to wood shavings or wood chips is that they are not really absorbent so your hamster's toilet area will need cleaning regularly unless you train them to use a litter tray. It also isn't as comfortable to lie on as some other materials so you may want to use something different in their sleeping area.

There is some controversy about wood shavings and wood chips and many people will say avoid using Cedar and Pine although the general consensus appears that UK Pine is safe. The reason for avoiding these softwoods is that they contain aromatic oils call Phenol which smell lovely to us but for your hamster who is breathing them in constantly it can irritate their sensitive little noses and cause respiratory issues. Some believe that the oils can be absorbed into the hamster's body leading to liver and neurological damage.

If choosing wood shavings or wood chips go with a safe hardwood like Aspen or if you're in the UK Spruce is more widely used. Try to buy from a pet store or if purchasing online then a reputable company that are selling them specifically for use in hamster cages rather than from a hardware store because the wood should then have been treated so they don't contain mites or other parasites.

Wood Pulp

This is more environmentally friendly and hamster aware than wood shavings or wood chips. The pulp looks a bit like grey shredded cabbage. If purchasing this check that it is labelled as being free from hydrocarbons which are the dangerous Phenol oils mentioned above. The good thing about wood pulp is that it is very absorbent but is slightly more expensive than wood chips or wood shavings. It isn't as easy for hamsters to dig and sculpt so some people buy wood pulp to put on the bottom of their cage and mix wood shavings with it so that your hamster has two different types of material to play with.

Hay

This should only ever be bought from a pet shop as it will have been treated before being packaged. Never use hay that you have collected from the fields because it can contain mites which will irritate your hamster and can lead to skin conditions. Whilst it may be okay for a nesting material it isn't the best thing to use as bedding (substrate) as it can become tangled around their feet whilst digging and also they may start to confuse it with food. If you do use hay then check it regularly to make sure it's not mouldy.

Pellets

These can be made from wood, compressed vegetable or grain by products such as wheat grass or recycled paper. Pellets made from pine are okay to use as long as it has been heat treated and those made from recycled newspaper should be non-toxic and biodegradable so always make sure you check the packaging or description before buying.

Pellets don't scatter as much as wood shavings or wood chips (better for wire cages) and are more absorbent. They are also slightly better at odour control.

The disadvantages are they are dustier and harder on your hamster's feet and not very comfortable for them unless you pay a bit more and find the softer ones but even then there are better alternatives.

Corn Cobs

These are ground down to a fine and granulated material and tend to be a mustard colour. Whilst I've listed them because they are an option that some people choose I wouldn't personally recommend them as they are not very absorbent and it is tempting for your new pet to eat them. They can also go mouldy which isn't good for your pet's health and will mean more cleaning for you. As with the pellets, they aren't as comfortable for your hamster either and as they are going to be spending all their lives in it I, personally, would opt for something different.

Shredded Paper

This is most used as a nesting material and is easy to make yourself. Basically you just need to cut soft paper such as toilet paper, paper towels, facial tissues or plain paper into long strips. It should be non-toxic and contain no ink. Bear in mind that commercial paper can be coated for resilience so even when it has been shredded it's not very comfy for your hamster so I would recommend using softer types such as toilet paper or tissues. Also never use newspaper because it is covered in potentially toxic and grubby newsprint which can rub off onto your hamster's fur and can be an irritant as well as putting them at risk of ingesting it when they clean themselves.

For nesting material, paper is great but as a bedding material it's not so good because it isn't as absorbent (other than paper towels which aren't as soft) It's also not as economical as some of the other options for a bedding material as if you are providing your Roborovski with a deep layer it means you will need to shred up a lot of paper which will take a long time and as it will get damp very quickly you will need to change it often which makes it fairly expensive. It's also not the best material for digging in.

White Cellulose Fibre
This is becoming more popular with hamster owners as it doesn't contain ink, dyes or chemicals. It is extremely absorbent, soft, hypoallergenic and has no scent that will irritate your hamster's tiny nose. There are many different brands out there and whilst some people say it is expensive, if you buy in bulk and do a good job at spot cleaning so you can go longer between whole bedding changes it can actually work out quite economical.

What To Avoid

Scented Material
As well as pine and cedar wood as mentioned above you should also avoid any wood or material that is scented. Whilst this can smell lovely and disguise the odour of your hamster's cage they often contain chemicals that will irritate your hamster's little nose and respiratory system and your hamster can be allergic to scented products.

Dusty Material
Your hamster will constantly be digging around in its cage so dusty materials will mean that they are kicking up fine particles that can irritate their eyes and nose leading to inflammation and repeated sneezing and their respiratory system can easily become blocked by dust. Avoid any dusty materials including sawdust.

Cat Litter
Hamsters are coprophagic which means they eat their own faeces to gain nourishment and aid the digestion process. Not only can the chemicals in cat litter be toxic but many of them are designed to clump when wet which can cause a blockage if your hamster ingests them and this internal obstruction can lead to death.

Straw

This has sharp ends which can cause your hamster injury, especially if they store it in their delicate cheek pouches. There are special, soft, flattened lengths of barley straw available on the market now which is sold for the purpose of using in hamster cages but I would recommend only using these in their sleeping houses and only if you are absolutely certain they are safe.

Long Fibres

Synthetic forms of bedding such as polyester fibres can tangle around their limbs and cut off circulation so never use long, stringy materials such as wool, cotton or anything that can split and wind its way around your hamster's legs or feet. Coconut fibres are sometimes used in cages but these can be sharp and hurt their little feet so it would be better to avoid.

Indigestible Material

Cotton wool/cotton balls, polyester stuffing, felt and anything similar should all be avoided because they are hard to digest and can cause problems with their digestive systems. They can also get stuck and compacted in their cheek pouches, stomach or intestines.

Considerations

Your hamster is going to spend its whole life in its bedding and nesting material so choose one that is soft, absorbent and suitable for hamsters. Not only will it make your pet happy and healthy saving you money in vet bills but will also make it easier for you when it comes to cleaning – the better the bedding the less often you will have to do full bedding changes.

Whilst you can buy colourful bedding and nesting material which looks really pretty, white is often better because soiled bedding is easier to see and remove making your cage cleaner and if your hamster is ill or bleeding you will spot it straight away.

Roborovski Hamsters love to dig and tunnel underground so it is recommended that the bedding on the bottom of the cage is around 7.5 centimetres (3 inches) deep but a 15 centimetre (6 inches) layer would be appreciated and make your hamster very happy. Yes, more bedding may cost more in the short term but actually if you are savvy about cleaning your cage (see next chapter) then having a deeper layer means you will need to do fewer full bedding changes.

You can make your own bedding and nesting material but whilst it's perfectly fine to cut toilet paper or tissue, et cetera into strips, I wouldn't recommend trying to make your own paper pulp, pellets, wood chippings or any other type of bedding material unless you do in depth research on the right materials to use and have the necessary equipment and time to make bedding that is suitable and safe. Often it is quicker, easier and cheaper to buy in bulk rather than spending the time making your own.

Your hamster will often nibble on their bedding but even if they don't it can still be digested if it sticks to their food – for example, hay can stick to wet apple slices. Always read the label of any products you buy and make sure it is completely safe for your hamster before purchasing.

Chapter 5: Hamster Accessories

Inside The Cage

As well as bedding and nesting materials there are also other essentials that need to be included inside your hamster's cage.

Water Bottle

This is an absolute must have as even though your hamster may not drink a lot, they can get dehydrated very quickly. Hamster bottles are usually the vacuum action, inverted type that can be hung from the side of the cage and work by releasing the water as the hamster drinks from it. Always ensure it is suitable for a Roborovski Hamster and is placed low enough that your pet can reach it easily. Water should be fresh every day and the bottle should be checked regularly – a common problem is that these bottles malfunction and leak or can get blocked which not only means the hamster can become dehydrated as they have no water to drink but can also result in wet bedding that is uncomfortable and is at risk of going mouldy if it isn't dried out or removed.

If you have an aquarium style cage then it is not possible to attach them to the cage but you can buy water bottles especially for this purpose – always ask in the pet store or check the details on the website if buying online to make sure that you're buying one that is suitable. Usually these are attached by suction cups although many people recommend against using these as they don't last as long. Other options include those with loops that can be attached to the lid of your cage or ones that hook over the sides of the aquarium.

You can use a water dish and many people say that hamsters do enjoy drinking from this but as they will also defecate in it and put bedding and food inside, it can become dirty very quickly and can cause your hamster to become ill. If you do use a water dish I would advise you clean it out at least three times a day and also use it in conjunction with a water bottle.

Always make sure it is shallow so your hamster doesn't drown in it and keep a close eye on them because if they climb in and get wet but aren't dried properly then they can catch cold which, left untreated, can be fatal for a Roborovski Hamster.

Food Dish

These need to be small and shallow so the hamster can get to the food but also heavy so it can't be tipped over. A hamster will generally climb inside their food bowl so make sure it's big enough for them to comfortably sit in whilst eating. Ceramic or porcelain is a great option as your hamster cannot chew them. Although you don't have to buy an expensive hamster dish always make sure that whatever you purchase is suitable for your hamster, allows them easy access to food and cannot be destroyed by their teeth. (Remember plastic can be chewed).

Exercise Wheel
Other than their food and water dish, an exercise wheel is the most important item to provide your Roborovski Hamster with. These are the most active hamsters and will love to run. Unfortunately as you cannot provide your pet with acres and acres of land in which to runabout in providing an exercise wheel is the next best thing – think of it as the hamster equivalent of a treadmill at the gym.

A hamster wheel will either have one side open and one side closed whilst others have both sides covered with just a small opening cut out for your hamster to slip through. The former is the most common but whichever you choose is really just preference – if you want to see your hamster run then you may prefer one with an open side but they may be happier to be enclosed whilst they run.

I would recommend that you consider the noise factor when you purchase your hamster wheel. If the cage is in your bedroom or the lounge for instance, then you are not going to appreciate a squeaky or noisy wheel constantly spinning whilst you are trying to sleep or watch TV and it can quickly become irritating. Therefore it is worth spending a little bit more and buying a silent one with ball bearings which gives it a smooth, quiet spin. They can be purchased for under £15. (Less than $20 in the US).

Also ensure that your hamster wheel is solid rather than having rungs. When your Roborovski is whizzing around on his wheel it is easy for him to slip and fall through the gaps or get a tiny limb trapped. Some hamster cages will come with a wheel and this usually will have open rungs. If you decide to keep this hamster wheel you can weave some card or thick paper strips in and out of the rungs to make the surface gap free.

When choosing a wheel always make sure you get one that is large enough for your hamster to run comfortably – one that is too small can cause their backs to become arched – yet small enough that they won't struggle to move it. If you have two hamsters either buy two wheels or buy a bigger one so that they can run together. Usually 15-12 centimetres (or 6.5 inches) is the recommended size. 12 centimetres (or anything less than 6 inches) is far too small even for these tiny creatures.

The final factor to consider with a hamster wheel (who knew there was so much to think about with such a simple item!) is how it will fix into your cage. There are two options; those that attach to the side of the cage which is fine if you are using one with wire bars or those that come with a stand, better suited for an aquarium style enclosure. Always check before you buy to make sure you are getting the one that is best suited to your cage set up and your hamster.

Toys

These are often brightly coloured pieces of plastic resembling toddler toys although many can be made from wood. There are so many on the market I could write a whole book just on hamster toys! Toys are super important as they give your hamster something to think about and prevent boredom – a hamster that is happily playing with toys and getting exercise has less time to try to solve the problem of how to escape it's cage or open the door to its enclosure. As well as keeping it busy toys will also give your hamster much needed exercise, keeping them fit and active which means not only are they less likely to become overweight but should have less medical problems leading to a longer life.

Popular toys include miniature houses with numerous opening and slanted roofs for the hamster to climb. They usually resemble houses that you would find out in the real world.

Logs are another good choice. These can be hollowed out like coconut shells and be used as covered bridges for your hamster to hide beneath or can be tube like with numerous holes for your hamster to pop in and out of.

For Roborovski Hamsters who naturally love to climb and scurry up and down objects a flexible ladder is perfect. Adding platforms, climbing bars and suspension bridges can provide extra challenges to keep your hamster interested especially if you buy the type that can be configured to make different pathways. Flexible items that can bend around other toys can make it more fun and you can fix several together to make one long run around the cage which is great if your enclosure is all on one level as not only does it give your hamster the opportunity to climb but also allows you to maximise the space you have in the enclosure. Just ensure that the hamster can't climb up a ladder or onto a platform and hop over the side of the cage!

Hamsters, even those born in captivity, will naturally want to burrow so they will love objects that give them the feeling of tunnelling and burrowing and these will make your hamster cage resemble the type of home your pet would have had in the wild. As well as alleviating boredom, plenty of tunnels will also make your new friend feel secure.

Oversized plastic fruit is great for your hamster to hide and sleep in, as are geometric shapes such as globes, cubes and hexagons. The latter often connect to slides, tunnels and other shapes enabling you to make a large playground for your hamster.

Other toys included seesaw and wooden barrels.

Hamster toys can get expensive, especially if you are buying lots that connect together. However you don't have to always go to the pet shop or buy online, you can easily make toys out of pretty much anything. For instance, toilet paper tubes make great tunnels and can be placed underneath the bedding. Soup tins (as long as they don't have any sharp edges are great for your hamster to climb in and out of. Ladders from broken toys or the sort you buy for bird cages can often be suitable for Roborovski Hamsters. Cardboard boxes, Lego, egg cartons (cardboard not Styrofoam), baskets, wooden cotton reels, paper chains and so on can all make brilliant toys. Just remember to check every one each day and remove once they become chewed or damaged.

Fruit tree branches can also make great toys and alder, maple, ash, apple tree and willow are all safe as long as they haven't been treated and are free from chemicals and pesticides.

Whatever toys you are thinking of using always remember the following:

Do not put in any toys that have sharp edges, splintery sides or use soluble dyes.

Wood should be untreated as the hamster will more than likely gnaw on it. Whilst this is good because it is a way of keeping their teeth healthy, be prepared to replace toys often.

Check plastic toys because if your hamster is chewing big pieces of plastic this can be harmful to them – whilst they probably won't digest a large amount it can still be harmful and can lead to the toy becoming sharp and leading to an injury.

Always make sure that the toys are sturdy and secured properly in the cage to prevent your hamster knocking them over and hurting themselves or falling when they are climbing.

To keep your hamster interested you should have a wide variety of toys and circulate them so they don't get bored of the same ones. Three or four toys in their enclosure at any one time is enough otherwise you risk filling your enclosure up so much they don't have any space to run around or burrow.

One last thing to remember is that wooden toys will absorb urine so should be changed when they are old and smelly. Plastic toys should be given a thorough wash every four to six weeks or whenever you do your whole cage clean.

Sand Bath

As I mentioned earlier, hamsters are naturally clean animals and you may often see your pet grooming itself. Sand is naturally abrasive so in the wild a Roborovski Hamster will roll around in it to clean the grease and odour from its fur. Although many consider a sand bath not to be a necessity I think it is a nice accessory to include in your hamster home. Not only will it help your hamster keep clean but will also provide it with a fun activity that it enjoys.

The sand that you use is very important, some will advise to use children's play sand although I would recommend you use one that is specifically made for small animals like Chinchillas or Hamsters so that you can be certain it has had anything bad eliminated, is bacteria free and is the correct size for your hamster.

To make a sand bath simply put a small amount of sand in a dish, bowl or jar (placed on its side) and place it in the cage. As your hamster will dig around and spray the sand everywhere keeping it to one side or in a corner will keep your housekeeping duties to a minimum. Make sure the container is wide enough so that your hamster can sit inside comfortably and turn around in (especially if you are using something like a jar that only has one opening).

Litter Box
Again, this isn't a necessity but is a preference. I would always recommend one because a litter box will confine any mess to one place and make it easier to clean your cage thereby stopping ammonia build up and prevent your cage hamster's home becoming smelly.

Use hamster litter if possible as this will be suitable for your pet and either buy an actual hamster litter tray or make one from a plastic container or cardboard box. A home made one will need to be replaced more often than a shop bought one so I would recommend you purchase a commercial hamster litter tray if possible.

Once you have discovered where your pet urinates and defecates place the litter box there. You only need enough litter to cover the bottom of the container. As hamsters will usually just use one spot as the toilet area they will naturally go back to the same place. If your hamster doesn't recognise the box as a litter tray at first put in some soiled bedding and place your hamster on top. Eventually it will associate the smell and the spot with the toilet and will start to use the litter tray. Don't force your Roborovski to use the toilet otherwise you may end up putting them off it altogether as they could associate it with fear.

If you find your hamster isn't using the litter box for its intended purpose then you may have to consider why. For instance, is the enclosure big enough? If your hamster is sleeping in the litter tray then maybe this is a sign that it doesn't like the sleeping house you have given it or if it is hiding food there then maybe there isn't enough hiding places in which case add more tunnels and hidey holes.

If the cage is too big (or you have more than one hamster) then you may have more than one toilet spot; if this is the case simply place a litter box in each one.

Eventually your hamster should start to co-operate but will do so in their own time. If they are using the box to urinate but not to poop then simply pick the pellets up and flush them down your own toilet.

Outside The Cage

You may occasionally want to let your Roborovski out of its cage so that it can have a bit more space to explore. Of course, unlike a cat or a dog you can't just let them roam free around the house or even one room as they would just run and hide and you may never see them again. However there are some ways that you can let your hamster out whilst still keeping them safe.

Hamster Balls

In my opinion this is another must have item. It is a great way to allow your Roborovski to leave their cage without getting injured or lost. These comprise of an acrylic container which splits into two halves. You simply place your hamster inside, close up the sides and watch him go.
The only downside with these hamster balls is that they have no ventilation or access to water so I don't recommend you keep your hamster in one for more than fifteen minutes or less if it is a hot day and never leave them alone. Always keep these hamster balls out of direct sunlight otherwise your pet can overheat.

Whenever your hamster is roaming around in a ball make sure it is in a wide open space so it can't get hurt and keep the door closed (need I say keep it away from stairs?) Always make sure the room is quiet and there are no other pets roaming around. Remember your Roborovski Hamster isn't a toy so don't let children play alone with them whilst they are in these balls – it is very tempting to a child to roll the ball around which can make the animal very disorientated.

Play Box or Habitat Trail

Another safe way of letting your hamster explore a new environment yet still staying safe is to make a play box or a habitat trail.

Find a large (the bigger the better) cardboard box or plastic container and put down a layer of bedding. A habitat trail differs slightly from a play box in that you make lots of tunnels for your hamster to run about in – kind of like a big maze whereas a play box is filled with toys, more like an adventure playground for your hamster.

Once you've made your play box or habitat trail then let your hamster loose. Just make sure that they can't climb out and once again put any other pets in a separate room.

Always place toys in the center of the box and make sure you supervise your pet – you will be surprised at how quickly your crafty critter can climb toys and escape.

Whenever your hamster is outside its cage always close the door of the room it is in (as well as any windows) just in case they do manage to get out.

Chapter 6: Feeding

Hamsters, like people, are omnivorous which means they have a varied diet comprising both plant and animal matter. In the wild hamsters will eat whatever is available seasonally such as wheat, soybeans, barley and peas, root vegetables such as potatoes and carrots as well as plants, leaves and flowers. They will also catch insects and other invertebrates such as spiders, mealworms, moths and crickets.

You may be a bit squeamish and not want to give your hamster any insects although should you wish to do so then mealworms as a treat are a good option as they are high in protein. Just be aware that if you have the type of enclosure with open wire bars you may not want to put in live insects as these can quite easily escape.

Seed Mixes
The bulk of your Roborovski Hamster's diet should be comprised of a hamster mix as these should cover all of its basic nutritional needs. These mixes do vary in the type of ingredients used so I would always recommend spending a bit more money and buying a more expensive one as this is more likely to be better quality and therefore healthier for your hamster. As Roborovski Hamsters are so tiny they only need about a teaspoon of this mix a day so it will last a long time.

Typically these hamster mixes will include corn, grains, alfalfa, seeds, beans, dried fruit and dried vegetables such as dehydrated carrots or peas, peanuts and sunflower seeds. As the latter two ingredients are high in fat they should only be given in small quantities therefore try to choose a mix that is low on these ingredients otherwise your hamster is at risk of becoming obese.

Some mixes are just made for hamsters in general so be careful when purchasing and ensure you only buy one that is suitable for Roborovski Hamsters because these will contain smaller seeds. Should you buy one that is generic and intended for Syrian Hamster the seeds may be far too big for your tiny pet.

Seed mixes offer good flavours and a variety and also give the hamster the opportunity to forage and select their food in a similar way to how they would in the wild. However one problem that often arises is that hamsters will most likely pick out the seeds that it prefers and ignore the ones that it isn't so keen on – usually the less healthy sunflower seeds and peanuts are invariably the ones that are chosen whilst the rest are hidden so you may think that your hamster is getting a well-balanced diet when in fact it isn't therefore it is important to keep an eye on your hamster's weight and appetite levels. You can avoid your hamster only eating its favourite foods by monitoring what it picks out and then not feeding those for a few days. For instance, if you notice it only likes the nuts then pick these out before giving them the feed; this way they won't have a choice but to eat the rest of the ingredients.

Seed mixes are colourful and whilst they look more appealing you can buy food pellets or food blocks which often have the same combination of grains, fruits and vegetables that a seed mix would but are ground up, compressed and chopped into cubes or small pellet shapes. Whilst these are not as much fun for your hamster they do include all the nutrients they need therefore you may want to consider using these if you are worried about your hamster picking out it's favourite food all the time. Even if you use a mix most of the time I would recommend you add a food cube every now and then because they do encourage gnawing and therefore is a good way to ensure your hamster's teeth are worn down correctly.

Whilst you can make your own hamster mix using seeds, grains and nuts found in health food stores it is usually easier and cheaper to just buy a commercial hamster food mix and this way you can be confident that your pet is receiving the right balance of nutrients.

Fruit And Vegetables
Your Roborovski Hamster needs a varied diet and although the commercially bought seed mixes are a good start and should comprise the main bulk of their diet you should also supplement them with fruits and vegetables. Hamsters enjoy new tastes and so new food is another way to alleviate boredom. Cut fruits and vegetables into small, manageable pieces but don't blend them as chewing is good for your hamster. Don't put in the whole amount of fruit or vegetable, for example, don't give your hamster a full apple or a whole carrot cut up (or even a whole slice) but rather just two or three tiny pieces (around fingernail size) that they can comfortably hold between their paws. Remember what is a small amount to you is a huge feast for them.

Always make sure you rinse the fruits and vegetables in water and let them sit at room temperature to dry off before giving them to your pet.

Fruit and vegetables need to be free of pesticides so if you are unsure don't use any that are wild.

The following are acceptable fruits and vegetables to feed to your Roborovski Hamster. There may be many others that aren't included here (good and bad food lists are constantly being updated) so if you want to give your hamster something that isn't on this list then feel free to do a quick Google search to see if it is suitable.

Good fruit options include seedless apples, grapes, bananas, peaches, blackberries, strawberries, blueberries, cranberries, plums, dates, figs, cherries and melon. If you want to be a bit more exotic than lychee, kiwi fruit, cantaloupe, Logan berries and mango are good. Raspberries and raspberry leaves are also suitable with the latter being helpful if your Roborovski Hamster has Diarrhoea

Remember fruit needs to be seedless and free from stones and pits. Never give apple core or apple pips to your hamster as these are poisonous to them.

Some people claim that the leaves and green parts of the strawberry are toxic to hamsters so I would always play it safe and remove these.

Suitable vegetable choices include asparagus, broccoli, cabbage (but in limited amounts) carrot, sweetcorn, cucumber (good to avoid dehydration especially when your hamster is out of its cage) green beans, peas, parsnips, celery, spinach, sweet bell peppers, asparagus, courgettes (or zucchini if you're in America) lettuce, bean sprouts, cauliflower (leaves and stalks) kale, squash and sweet potatoes, turnip and water cress Both water chestnuts and chestnuts are fine for your hamster.

Other suitable foods include dandelion leaves, clover, coriander, endive, fenugreek, basil, chicory and Chinese leaves.

There is some dispute over celery with people saying that it chokes hamsters to death. I feel if cut up small this avoids them becoming too stringy and should be fine but would always say let your common sense prevail, if you are uncertain about any type of food then just don't feed it.

Lettuce is another one that people disagree over because it doesn't contain high nutritional value for your hamster and can be watery but every now and then should be fine.

Many people will say don't feed fruit and vegetables to your Roborovski Hamster because they contain too much sugar which causes Diabetes. Whilst this is true, Roborovski Hamsters aren't as prone to Diabetes as some of the other Dwarf species such as Campbell's or Winter Whites so a little bit of fruit won't be harmful and will add variety into their diet however always feed in moderation.

Other people will say that fruits are too watery especially cucumber and this can give them stomach upsets and diarrhoea. Again, I'm not disputing this but in moderation, for example, a slice of cucumber twice a week, should not make your hamster ill.

Other Food And Treats
Roborovski Hamsters can eat meats as well such as cooked ground beef that has been rinsed well in hot water in order to remove the grease and steamed or baked turkey or chicken. They can also eat cooked Cod fish with the bones and skin removed.

As mentioned above, in the wild they will eat insects which you can pick up in the pet shop such as Grasshoppers, Mealworms and Crickets. Don't feed wild caught insects as these can contain pesticides which could make your hamster ill.

Well cooked eggs either boiled or scrambled, plain tofu and plain low fat yoghurt are also good for your hamster.

Adult Roborovski Hamsters can be given the occasional treat such as cheese. However you must make sure you are feeding one that is safe for your hamster as lots of cheeses are high in saturated fat as well as containing lots of added salt and flavourings. Ideally, as an occasional treat, a teaspoon of low-fat unflavoured cottage cheese is the best.

Brown or wholemeal bread, linseed, rye bread or organic bread with seeds embedded in the crust all make great treats for your hamster. The crust which most of us throw away is the best part for your hamster. Bread soaked in milk is also a perfect food for pregnant or nursing females, babies and elderly hamsters with weak teeth.

Hamsters love nuts and as well as being an excellent protein source they contain no cholesterol and very little amounts of saturated fat making them a fantastic snack. Walnuts, pecans, cashew nuts, hazelnuts, pistachios and peanuts are all great choices but make sure they are unflavoured and unsalted. Giving nuts to your hamster whilst they're still in their shell will provide your hamster with both a treat and a puzzle for them to solve which can help avoid boredom. Depending on how strong your hamster is and how tough the nut is, they may struggle to open the shell in which case you could partly open it for them.

Peanuts are controversial because they contain Aflatoxin which can be harmful but only if given in large amounts.

Peanut Butter can be given as a treat but only in VERY TINY amounts as it is fattening and sticky (which isn't great for being stored in cheek pouches). The best choice would be organic peanut butter that has no added salt, sugar or flavourings and is usually found in health food shops or online.

Dried fruits are another good treat but just remember they are high in sugar so should be fed sparingly. Raisins as well as banana, strawberries, papaya, honeydew, figs, raspberries, melon, cherries and blackberries can all be bought dried in both pet shops and online.

One piece of plain, unflavoured, unsalted and unsweetened popcorn is a great treat. Popcorn still has all the health benefits and nutrients as ordinary corn but please don't give any popcorn that has just been freshly cooked and is hot as it could burn their mouth.

Hamsters are natural seed eaters as this is something they will eat in the wild and they contain many nutrients. Sunflower seeds, wheat seeds, sesame seeds, flax seeds and pumpkin seeds will all be enjoyed however a word of caution about pumpkin seeds as they can have tough shells and large kernels which your tiny Roborovski might struggle with.

Dog biscuits can be given as well as long as they don't contain garlic, onion or onion powder and you will find these are provided at hamster shows.

Foods To Avoid
Tomatoes are very acidic so it is not recommend you feed these.

Watermelon contains too much water so again, should be avoided as it can cause diarrhoea and tummy upsets. Don't even feed the skin, rind or pips.

White bread should not be given because it is thought that the flour is highly processed and refined which can mean your hamster can convert it into sugar leading to health problems. White bread has very little nutritional value and the other types of bread listed above make far better alternatives.

Almonds are another one to avoid as they can contain a cyanide substance that is poisonous to hamsters. Some people will say that sweet almonds are fine but I again I would play it safe and not feed them any because there are plenty of other nuts available.

Processed and flavoured cheese such as Stilton and Blue Cheese should all be avoided as they can be toxic to hamsters.

Hamsters should not be given any citrus fruits such as oranges as they are highly acidic. Mandarin and pineapple should also be avoided for the same reason.

Chocolate should not be given to your hamster, as well as being full of saturated fat and sugar it also contains a chemical called Theobromine which can be toxic and deadly to hamsters and other animals as they cannot metabolise it so it remains in their system for twenty four hours, effectively poisoning the hamster.

Other foods that should be avoided include fruit stones such as apricot and cherry stones, seeds such as apple and grape seeds, peach leaves, tinned (canned) foods, sweets (candy), chips, crisps and so on.

Kidney beans, ordinary potatoes and rhubarb are another one that appears to be controversial with some owners saying don't feed at all and others saying they are okay if cooked. One thing that is agreed upon is that you should never feed these raw.

Avocados are another one that some people will say are fine in small quantities as long as they are peeled however they do have a substance that has been linked to heart attacks in small creatures such as hamsters, if fed in large quantities.

How To Feed
You can either put food directly in a bowl for your hamster to munch on or you can scatter it around the cage. Some owners will say that this is pointless as hamsters will enjoy scattering the food around themselves however what hamsters actually do is hoard the food and find places to hide it where they can return to it later, rather like squirrels with their nuts. I feel that scattering food around the cage encourages their foraging instinct and can provide a fun, enjoyable activity which alleviates boredom. I won't recommend one over the other as its personal preference but I think a combination of both works fine. You may prefer to hide and scatter dry food like carrot, seeds and nuts and keep the softer, wet foods like cucumber and fruits in the bowl so as to keep your cage a bit cleaner. (Although this can be redundant if your Roborovski Hamster is depositing it's food around the cage anyway).

Any uneaten food should be removed within a few hours otherwise it runs the risk of going bad or mouldy which can be harmful to your pet. Make sure you search the cage thoroughly to find any that your hamster has stored away.

Constantly changing your Roborovski Hamster's diet is harmful and can cause stomach problems and diarrhoea. Try to stick to the same dry food if possible and introduce new foods slowly. It is always a good idea to introduce a food one day then have a day or two with just hamster mix before introducing another food.

You will need to keep an eye on how much your hamster eats and drinks, again another problem with hoarding as you may be tricked into thinking they are eating more than they are. If you notice that there is more food in their bowl than usual or they aren't drinking much, they appear to lose weight or their droppings are moist or hindquarters are soiled then take your hamster to the vet immediately. A good way to keep a check on the amount they drink is to put marks on the side of the water bottle.

Wet and powdered food should not be given to your hamster unless directed to by the vet, for instance if your pet has a dental problem then this type of food may be recommended. If your hamster is sick and requires wet food then you will need to make sure that the food dish is cleaned out thoroughly and fresh food is given at least twice a day as this type of food can go mouldy quickly.

One final point I will make is that with any item on the safe foods list should all be given in moderation. In large quantities any one of those foods can be harmful either due to toxins, high sugar, salt, fat and so on. Hamsters need a variety of food in their diet but much like with humans too much of a good thing can have an adverse effect so always use common sense.

Chapter 7: Cleaning

Hamsters are very clean creatures and will naturally choose one area (or sometimes two if you have a large cage) to use for toileting. This makes it far easier for you to clean because you can just take the soiled bedding from this corner and replace it rather than cleaning the whole cage on a weekly basis.

Hamster poops are simply dried up pellets. They don't smell but do make the cage look untidy. The odour in your hamster's cage will be from their scent glands and the ammonia vapours from their urine. This is a harsh smell and a severe irritant for your hamster that relies on their sense of smell more than their eyesight. Urine can be detrimental to their health as it can irritate their eyes and respiratory tract. Hamsters that already have a chronic respiratory condition can be made worse if regularly exposed to these ammonia vapours. Any hamster, healthy or not, can be more susceptible to other infections if their enclosures are infrequently cleaned and they are constantly living in dirty, moist, bedding.

How often your hamster's house should be cleaned is an issue that is widely debated. Many people say a full bedding change once a week or once a fortnight is sufficient. I believe that how often you clean out your hamster's home depends on the type of housing you're using, how good you are at spot cleaning and how deep their bedding is. Everyone's set up is different so the information provided here is based purely on my own research and experience and may not be suitable for everybody.

I disagree with the full bedding change. I think that this is unnecessary because if you have a large cage with a 15 centimetre (6 inch) layer in your hamster's cage, how much of this is actually getting dirty? Think about it – your hamster walks and defecates only on the top layer. Not only that but as they usually choose one area to use as a toilet then this is the main area that will be soiled. (New hamsters may take a while to settle into a routine therefore you may need to clean more often at first.) If you train your hamster to use a litter tray then cleaning is even easier.

I recommend that you spot clean every day which simply means removing any wet or soiled bedding and poops, wiping down their wheel if the hamster wees on it and clean out the litter tray or sand bath if you use either of them.

Every four weeks you should do a full cage clean. Remove all toys and bedding – throw out the soiled and wet bedding and put the bottom layer into a separate bag. Wipe down the whole cage with a hamster safe disinfectant then clean all the toys. Make sure the enclosure is fully dry before you put fresh bedding into the bottom then put the older, clean bedding that you took out earlier.

Hamster's become very stressed when they have clean, fresh bedding because it no longer has the same smell which can confuse them. By only taking out soiled bedding and keeping the older, clean material it means that their enclosures will always smell the same. Not only is your hamster happy but you will also save money because you're not throwing out bedding just for the sake of it.

Of course if your cage is smelly or looks dirty then you may need to clean more often. If you have more than one hamster in the same cage then this may also require more frequent cleaning.

When doing a full cage clean your hamster will need to be removed. Put them in another temporary cage or even better, inside a hamster ball as this will give them exercise and keep them happy whilst you are busy cleaning. If you have young children or other pets that roam the house, such as dogs or cats, make sure they are in a separate room away from your hamster whilst they are out of their cage.

Chapter 8: Settling In And Taming

Before you can tame your new pet you will need to give it time to adjust to its new surroundings before even attempting to handle it. A new home will be stressful enough without adding human interaction and a Roborovski Hamster is more likely to respond positively once it is comfortable with its new surroundings. If your hamster is fearful when it first arrives then handling it will mean it could start to associate your scent with fear and this will make it very difficult, if not impossible, to tame.

Settling In

Once you have purchased your hamster you should take them home as soon as possible. If you are driving try to take the quickest route which will provide the smoothest journey. If you are walking try to go at a steady pace and try not to jostle the hamster container too much.

Hopefully you will already have its cage set up in a nice quiet room. Hamsters need a comfortable, clean place to live that is dry and free of draughts so they can sleep and rest peacefully. These creatures are very sensitive to ultrasound - high frequency noises which we cannot hear – and it causes them a lot of stress. Make sure your hamster's cage is away from any items which generate this ultrasound such as computers, televisions, vacuum cleaners and sources of running water.

As soon as you get home put your hamster in their enclosure and add in the bedding from the travel cage so it has something that smells familiar. Add fresh food and water if you haven't already done so then leave the hamster alone.

This may seem cruel and most likely you will be itching to get your new pet out and play with it but a Roborovski Hamster needs to get to know it's new surroundings so by leaving them alone you are helping them feel safe and secure which will make taming more fun for both of you. This time by themselves will allow them to roam their cage without fear of predators – which is what your hamster will view you as, at least in the beginning.

Keep any other animals away from the cage and don't let any children in the room either. Spot clean the cage and provide fresh food and water but keep these tasks to a minimum and go about them as quickly and quietly as possible.

Don't worry if your hamster sleeps a lot in these first few days, it is perfectly normal and they are simply adjusting to their new surroundings as well as recovering from the stress and physical exertion of the journey to their new home.

You may start to see your new friend marking their territory by licking their body and rubbing themselves against the side of the cage and toys. This shows they are starting to settle in.

After a few days they should start to settle into a routine of burrowing, exercising, sleeping and eating and this is the time you can start to handle and tame.

Taming

Once your hamster has settled in begin taming by simply getting them used to your voice. Sit next to their cage and speak in a very quiet, happy tone. The subject doesn't matter, after all your hamster won't be conversing back but it will get them used to the sound of your voice so feel free to talk about your day. If you feel silly telling a hamster all your woes then you could sing to them instead, just make sure you do so quietly with no dramatic key changes.

Never wake your hamster just so you can handle it. It may be frustrating if your hamster is only awake when you are out or asleep but rousing them from their own sleep will make them feel on edge and they will never relax thereby causing unnecessary stress. At least in the beginning, your Roborovski will view you as a predator so you need to work around their schedule.

The best time for handling is early in the morning or evening when your hamster has woken up and is actively running about its cage or happily playing.

To start interacting place your hand in their cage and let them sniff at you. Hold a treat out for them and see if they will take it from you. Repeat daily. If your hamster runs and hides or refuses to come near you after five or ten minutes then give up, leaving a smaller treat in their food bowl.

It is perfectly normal for your hamster to sniff your hand or fingers then dart away. Be patient and wait for them to approach you again. Never be tempted to make a grab for your hamster. Some owners recommend this but I think this can just make your Roborovski more wary of you as they can mistake your hand for a hawk. Also because they are so ridiculously fast you could easily end up accidentally hurting your hamster.

If the hamster refuses to come near you or is just running manically around their cage then another way of catching them is by placing a treat in a toilet roll tube or a cup then when they are inside very carefully picking this up and placing it over a small box lined with a soft towel and some bedding on the floor. Very gently tip your hamster out into your hands. The reason for the box is that your hamster will most likely try to escape and if you are not used to handling such fast animals they will succeed. If you are knelt over a box that has a soft landing your hamster won't get injured if they do dive away. A bad fall could make them associate being handled with pain.

Your first few sessions should concentrate on getting them used to being in your hand and getting you used to their speed.

Offer treats but don't force your hamster to eat anything. Many people will say you can't train a Roborovski with food as they don't respond this way but many others disagree and say treats are always good. For the purpose of this book I have included the ways that I know other people have used to train their Roborovski Hamsters which is with treats they know their pets enjoy however if it refuses to eat anything at all then of course just leave it be.

Once they start to take a treat from your fingers, start to put one in the palm of your hand. Eventually they should stop trying to escape and you should be able to stroke them gently with one finger. Once calmed and used to handling they can be very gentle creatures.

As with any animal, patience is a virtue. If at first you don't succeed, try and try again. Okay, enough clichés but you get the idea, basically you won't be able to tame your hamster overnight, and it could take weeks if not months until your Roborovski Hamster is comfortable with you picking them up. These creatures are well known for not being sociable with humans so you will need lots and lots of handling sessions; shorter sessions several times a day is far better than one long session as your hamster will be less stressed and it will be less frustrating for you.

Of course if you have purchased your hamster from a breeder that handle their animals at a young age as opposed to a pet shop or a rescue centre then your hamster may already be used to humans and therefore will just need to get used to you which could be done in a matter of days. If you are a breeder it is a good idea to handle babies from around two and a half to three weeks old by picking them up once or twice a day.

Once tamed it is a good idea to handle and play with your hamster every day so it remains tame. Many people say if you keep more than one

Roborovski Hamster in a cage together then daily human contact isn't necessary although I would still recommend you do handle them on a regular basis because that way they will remain comfortable, otherwise you may have to start the whole process over again.

If your hamster is pregnant then don't try to tame or handle until after the litter is born.

Always move slowly and speak in a quiet voice. Never use a loud voice even if your hamster does something you don't like. Instead say no firmly and quietly and when it stops doing whatever you disapprove of give it a treat.

When trying to tame the room you are in should be very quiet so that you hamster won't startle or jump out of your hand. Young children shouldn't really be present as they can be loud and unpredictable.

Never let children handle these type of hamsters, they are far too fast and their main objective will be to squirm and escape. Children can become excited or scared at their speed and jumping and shrieking will frighten your hamster even more, once again associating human contact with fear.

Some people suggest wearing dark clothing such as navy blue or black whenever handling Roborovski Hamsters.

A tip to get your hamster used to your scent is to tear up some toilet paper or soft tissues and rub your scent on it. Roborovski Hamsters like this and will use it for their bedding thus getting used to your scent and associating it with a calm and quiet time.

If your hamster really can't be tamed then leave them alone. Roborovski Hamsters are very shy by nature and may just dislike human contact. You can still enjoy your pet by watching their antics in the cage and sometimes it is more enjoyable as at least you know they are happy and stress free. Many people will say that a Roborovski never actually enjoy handling but merely tolerate it. Whilst I agree with this and don't think you should ever force your hamster to be tamed I think it is a good idea to try and do this if only so that vet visits or administering medicine is easier.

Chapter 9: Medical Conditions

Roborovski Hamsters are generally a healthy breed and very rarely get sick. However when they are it can be difficult to treat because they are so small or illness can quickly become serious if not treated immediately.

Common Illnesses

There may be many health issues not listed here that can affect a Roborovski Hamster but for the purpose of this book I have only included the most common ones. This section should be used for reference purposes only. Always consult a vet if you think your hamster is unwell.

Mites

Signs include scratching a lot, bald spots, scabs, crusty skin, wet fur and pink flesh. Mites can often affect the ears giving them a crumpled appearance. You may be able to see the mites as little moving dots at the roots of their fur but they also burrow into the skin and eat dead skin, making your hamster itchy.

Anti-mite sprays and drops can be purchased over the counter from pet stores or online but it is always recommended that you check with a vet before administering this to your pet. This ensures that you are using it correctly and that it is safe for your hamster.

If your hamster has mites they can be contagious so if it is living with other hamsters you will need to remove the one that is affected. Clean and disinfect your cage thoroughly, spray with anti-mite spray and put down fresh bedding.

You will also need to spray your hamster as unless the anti-mite spray or liquid comes into contact with their skin then it won't be affective in ridding your Roborovski of mites. Always shield their eyes and heads when doing this.

Always wear gloves and wash your hand thoroughly with anti-bacterial soap afterwards as mites can bite humans causing welts although they cannot live on our skin.

Mange

This is a widespread infection of the skin and is characterised by excessive fur loss, redness and scaly skin. It can affect hamsters that are weak or old or can be caused by an advanced mite infection.

As above you will need to isolate your hamster if it doesn't live alone as mange is highly contagious. Clean and sterilise the cage it has lived in and change the bedding. If the dry and scaly skin is causing discomfort this can be relieved by rubbing olive oil on your hamster and this is harmless if it is ingested whilst your Roborovski is cleaning itself. However you will also need to consult a vet immediately because your hamster will need antibiotics and medication which is stronger than that bought over the counter.

Wet Tail

This is a bacterial infection caused by stress and symptoms include diarrhoea and dehydration. It is thought that stress stimulates the release of bacteria from the intestines and it is a disease that is more common in young hamsters. Amongst other things Wet Tail can be caused by dietary problems such as an unbalanced diet, malnutrition or weaning too early or stress factors such as too much handling at too young an age or unsanitary cage conditions.

Symptoms include a sticky wet backside, refusal to eat and drink, slow moving or inactive, unusually quiet.

If you believe your hamster is suffering from Wet Tail consult a vet immediately as antibiotics will be needed and these should be administered correctly. Roborovski Hamsters don't deal with this illness as well as other hamster species so the quicker you can get treatment the better chance they have of fighting the illness.

Keep the affected hamster in a quiet, warm environment away from stress. Again it is highly contagious so always quarantine the affected hamster.

Spinning

This is a genetic neurological defect that is apparent whenever the hamster is stressed or excited. It is more frequent in those hamsters that have been inbred or in certain bloodlines, for instance, it appears to affect the White Faced Robos more but whether this is linked to colour or a side effect of increased breeding no-one is certain.

You will know if your hamster has the Spinning illness as it will suddenly spin endlessly and uncontrollably around on its axis. Whilst it may look funny or cute at first it is a serious indication that something is wrong in their brain. If you don't notice it until your hamster is older then it could be a sign of a stroke or a tumour.

If the affected hamster is living with other Roborovski Hamsters then separate them immediately as a cage mate that is spinning uncontrollably can not only stress the others out but can also irritate them making the ill hamster more susceptible to attacks and preventing them from eating and resting.

Sadly there is no cure but symptoms can be minimised by providing them with a safe, quiet environment away from stress. Try to keep the hamster as occupied as much as possible as this can distract them so provide a hamster wheel and plenty of toys and handle them whenever possible.

If your hamster can lead a normal life and is able to eat, drink and play as normal then it is possible for them to continue as they are. However consider their quality of life and if it is spending more time spinning then anything else then it may be kinder to consider euthanizing your hamster. I would always recommend you visit the vet for advice and confirmation of the illness as soon as you spot any symptoms.

If you know your hamster is a spinner then please do not breed these hamsters as it can be passed on to the young. Even if your hamster only has a mild case of Spinning if bred there is a high chance of the offspring being more affected and having their quality of life reduced.

Diarrhoea
Roborovski Hamsters in the wild are susceptible to this due to the scarcity of vegetation in the wild.

In captivity causes include a poor diet or continuous changes to their diet, eating too many fruit and vegetables or eating rotten food, drinking dirty water or being kept in draughty or damp conditions.

Symptoms include runny poop and refusal to eat and drink.

To aid a hamster that has Diarrhoea feed them dry food such as bread, crisp bread, rice cakes and give them Camomile tea instead of water. However Diarrhoea can kill if not treated early enough so always consult a vet immediately.

Diarrhoea can be prevented by changing drinking water each day and removing old food that hasn't been eaten before it can go off. Only make changes to their diet gradually and introduce new foods one at a time. Raspberry leaves to chew on can also help.

Fighting Wounds

Whilst Roborovski Hamsters can live happily together sometimes they just decide to fight for no apparent reason. This can cause them to be bitten and scratched and as this can take place late at night when you are asleep you may not witness this behaviour therefore if you keep more than one Roborovski Hamster to a cage it is important that you check them regularly for any fighting wounds.

Roborovski Hamsters are quick healers and usually any damage is healed within a week and hair should have grown back within a week or two.

Clean, 'dust free' bedding can also aid healing but the dirty wound should also be disinfected gently with a cloth and clean boiled water. Don't use cream or ointment as when your hamster cleans itself it will lick it off and this could cause it to become ill. If you do use a cream then get it from the vet as they will recommend one that is safe and it will usually contain antibiotics to aid healing.

Always separate the injured so they can recover in peace, you can always reintroduce them properly at a later date.

Tumours and Abscesses

Compared to other hamster species tumours and abscesses are common in Roborovski Hamsters. Tumours can take the form of scent gland tumours in males, mammary tumours and lumps in neck or chin. They tend to be slow growing and don't spread externally but unfortunately because Roborovski Hamsters are so small it is impossible to operate on these tumours so there is no cure.

If you find a suspicious lump on your hamster always get it checked by the vet as although you may think it is a tumour it may just been an abscess. Your vet may use a fine needle to pierce the lump and observe the pus or analyse the cells to determine if it is indeed a tumour or an abscess whilst some vets will simply prescribe a course of antibiotics and if the lump reduces then it is clearly a tumour. Whilst this process of elimination may seem unnecessary it is usually kinder to treat your hamster with antibiotics first rather than give a needle which can put them at risk of cardia arrest due to their small size.

Whether tumour or abscess your hamster should be made to feel as comfortable as possible. Provide plenty of bedding and lots of hideaways and sleeping places. Monitor the growth as sometimes they can be scratched open and become infected.

Hamsters very rarely show pain so it is serious if they show any sign of discomfort. If you know your pet has a tumour, even one that is slow growing, that is causing it pain and discomfort it may be kinder to let them go then suffer.

Pyometra
This only affects females as it is an infection of the womb.

Signs include trouble walking, refusing to eat or drink, discharge from the vulva and appearing bloated.

Urgent treatment is needed in the form of antibiotics so always visit your vet as otherwise it can be fatal. Unfortunately Roborovski Hamsters are so small it is impossible to spay them so even when treated the infection can reappear.

Dehydration
This is another illness that is linked to stress but sometimes your Roborovski Hamster may just stop drinking water for no apparent reason.

Symptoms include hamster looking thinner or out of condition, being slower, having trouble walking or sitting in a hunched over position.

Always check that the spout on the water bottle is working and provide diced cucumber. If your house is multi-level then put it on the ground floor. Once your hamster nibbles on the cucumber it should solve its dehydration if it doesn't then it could be a sign that your hamster has another health problem therefore you should consult a vet.

Heart Problems
The symptoms of this include lethargy but heart problems such as heart disease, valve issues, murmurs and epilepsy are not really visible in small rodents and sometimes you won't know that the creature is seriously ill until it suddenly dies. There are lots of reports about Roborovski Hamsters being found in their cage looking like they are mid-run or on their hamster wheels a short time after being purchased.

Always avoid buying young hamsters that are worryingly calm and lethargic or not reacting quite how they should. Whilst a Roborovski can be tamed it should always have that running response and a normal healthy one will not freeze or remain asleep when picked up.

Respiratory Issues
Symptoms include noisy breathing, sitting hunched over and sucking their sides in and out when breathing. Always seek medical attention from the vet immediately as respiratory issues can quickly become serious.

Sometimes after the infection has cleared up your hamster may continue to breathe noisily due to scar tissue on their lungs or upper respiratory tract. If this happens then listen closely to the new sound and monitor them closely – should the noise of their breathing change it could signal another infection.

Allergies
Not every snuffle will signal an infection. Hamsters can become allergic to bedding such as wood shavings or paper bedding that has been dyed. Some food contains colouring that looks appealing to us but can cause your hamster to feel quite wretched. Cedar shavings are another irritant.

If they have a mild snuffle with dry eyes or eyes which are slightly weepy but have no other symptoms and don't appear to be struggling to breathe then it could be worth changing their bedding. Bad skin lesions, sneezing, scratching and dermatitis are also signs of an allergy.

It may only affect one hamster in the group but you will need to identify the cause immediately and change it for all of the hamsters as any one of them could become allergic at a later date.

Old Age
Whilst it's not technically an illness and of course nothing that you can prevent I have listed it here because many owners worry about their Roborovski Hamsters once they start to get older.

Roborovski Hamsters don't age gracefully and around twelve months they usually start to lose their hair around their back end. Males tend to become more stained around their scent glands whilst females who have produced a litter tend to lose hair from their chest area.

As well as the hair loss owners tend to worry because their aging hamster will start to eat and drink less and may become skinny or look like they are 'shrinking'. Whilst these can be signs of a medical issue if your hamster is playing happily and running around as normal then they are most likely just aging. If in doubt have a check up with a vet but otherwise no extra care is needed. If you have a multi-level cage and find that your hamster is struggling then you may need to put them into a single level enclosure to prevent them injuring themselves.

Vaccinations

There are currently no vaccinations available for any type of hamster that I am aware of. Whilst they can suffer from common medical issues there isn't a vaccine available for any of them. Instead keeping your cage clean and providing a safe environment, fresh food and clean water every day should be enough to keep your pet healthy. If any injuries or symptoms of illness occur then visiting the vet is the best way to go. If you are worried you can always go for regular health checks if your vet advises this.

Pet Insurance

Believe it or not it is possible to get your Roborovski Hamster insured. There are different types of cover such as illness or accident only and the price is largely dependent upon how much you paid for your pet and the insurer you choose. Be aware that insurers won't cover pets with pre-existing conditions and most won't cover pregnancy.

Whilst it is good that you can get your pet insured I would question whether it is worth it. If you are going to put your Roborovski Hamster into pet shows then maybe you might want to insure them but if they're just sat alone in a cage all day in optimum conditions and you only paid £5 for them, it could cost more over their life time to insure than a vet bill would be.

I would think carefully about it as it may be worth just putting so much money aside each month just in case something happened to your pet rather than paying an insurance company for a policy you may never benefit from.

Chapter 10: How To Find A Lost Hamster

Losing any pet can be devastating but I feel losing a Roborovski Hamster is especially panic-inducing because of their small size and speed. They literally could be anywhere.

Prevention is always better than cure as they say and it is always best to ensure your cage is escape proof before you even bring your hamster home. That said if you are reading this because you have lost your hamster then the last thing you want is a lecture on how you should have kept them safe so here is a list of what action to take so that you have a better chance of finding them.

Firstly shut all the doors and windows. Okay I'm hoping that you always keep doors and windows firmly closed in whichever room your hamster is in, at least whenever they are alone in their enclosure without supervision as even if your cage is completely escape proof there is always that slim possibility that they will escape. Maybe they'll chew through a bar or discover a way to unlatch the door. Maybe one of your clips fails or you forget to latch the door or the lid properly. Don't underestimate these creatures as they can be smart and don't automatically assume that your hamster can't reach a window just because it's high up. I've known Roborovski Hamsters that have climbed up blind cords or squeezed through the bars of their cage and shimmied up the curtains to reach an open window.

It is much easier to find a hamster that is trapped in one room so if you have shut the doors and windows before the creature escaped then the good news is that you have a much better chance of finding them.

If your doors weren't shut when your hamster escaped and you believe they may have got into another room then quickly run around the house and shut all the doors and windows. If you have large gaps under your door which your hamster could squeeze under then seal these up, for example, you could use books to block them up. The last thing you want is for your hamster to be having a tour of your home whilst you're frantically searching for it under the bed or wherever.

Make sure that any other pets are locked firmly away in their cages or if you have bigger animals like cats or dogs make sure they're outside or shut in a room that your hamster cannot have got into – you do not want your cat or dog finding your hamster before you!

If you have other family members in the house then warn them that the Roborovski Hamster has escaped, they can also keep a watchful eye out and will be less likely to accidentally step on your pet if they are on the look-out for it.

Find a torch then start in the room their cage is kept in and methodically search it. You need to stay calm for two reasons. Firstly, your hamster is so small that running around like a headless chicken shouting and screaming at the top of your voice, won't help. Secondly this behaviour will spook your hamster and they may be able to smell your fear, both of which will keep them in hiding.

Start by searching the area around their cage. Sometimes they just stay near home so if their cage is placed on top of a cupboard or a desk or whatever, check around and underneath and behind this piece of furniture.

If they aren't near their cage then start to check their favourite spots. Much like a toddler, Roborovski Hamsters tend to like hiding in the same place they've hidden before so if they have escaped previously start checking the spots that they went last time or think about any spots they may have gone if you let them loose in a hamster ball.

Good places to look include shoes and handbags, behind or underneath heavy furniture such as sofas, chairs, tables, desks, bookshelves, beds, wardrobes and so on. Check behind and underneath appliances such as your oven, fridge, freezer, washing machine, etc., if they are kept in a kitchen area. This is where the torch will come in handy.

Basically check anywhere that has a tiny hole or gap, they could squeeze through. Pull out drawers and check inside and behind. Also check pillows and pillow cases, cushions and blankets.

DO NOT push back any drawers or furniture too forcefully or too fast without thoroughly checking your hamster isn't behind or underneath it first. Always move slowly, carefully and quietly.

Whilst searching for gaps or good hiding spots also keep an eye out of anything that looks chewed. Some things can easily have a hole to squeeze through after a little bit of nibbling.

If you think that your hamster could be in more than one room then once you have methodically searched the room that they lived in move on to another. Hamsters tend to like bathrooms, especially ones that have lots of strong smelling shampoos, shower gels or perfume.

Roborovski Hamsters also like to be warm so another good place to look is near any heaters or radiators.

Another thing to look out for is food or poop trails. When you've got to go you've got to go and hamsters are not different. You may just well find a trail of tiny poops that could lead to your hamster's hiding place.

Before leaving their home they may have tucked food away in their cheek pouches so look for any food remains outside of the cage. If you keep any food in the room that they were living in – for instance some people keep a bag of sunflower seeds or hamster mix near their cages for easy access – check this food store as your hamster may well have discovered it and be hiding nearby or they may have stocked up and hidden a stash somewhere else. If you find any piles of food hidden in areas of your room then your hamster will no doubt be planning to return to them later.

If after checking every single nook and crevice then you may want to consider setting up a trap. I will say I hate traps *but* when it comes to lost hamsters they are usually fairly effective. Some owners will suggest humane mouse traps which don't hurt your hamster but they can occasionally malfunction so I recommend making your own container or bucket trap, if set up correctly your hamster will not be hurt and can be returned to their cage safely.

To make one of these 'traps' find a bucket or a container that is deep enough so your hamster can't climb out but not so deep that they will injure themselves falling into it.

Place something soft in the bottom such as a towel – I would probably add a layer of soft bedding or nesting material too just to cushion your hamster's fall. Inside place some lettuce or cucumber as when your hamster returns they may be thirsty, especially if they have been gone for a while. You may not notice that they have fallen into the bucket so cucumber or lettuce will also prevent them from becoming dehydrated if they're in there for a while.

Next make some steps or a ladder leading up to the top of the bucket. Before you start fashioning something complicated out of wood and nails or knotting bedsheets together these ladder or steps can be as simple as piling up toys or books.

Books are usually the quickest and easiest option and when you have made your steps leading all the way up to the top of the bucket, put a treat such as a sunflower seed or pumpkin seed on every step.

Inside the bucket place a special treat with a strong smell such as cheese or apple slices.

The idea is your hamster will be enticed by the smell of food and the treats on the steps as well as their enjoyment of climbing. They follow the trail to the top of the bucket and the treat inside will be so tempting they will happily jump into the bucket to get to it.

You can either stay in the same room but sit quietly in a corner or you can leave the room and shut the door firmly behind you, checking every so often to see if your hamster has reappeared. Whichever you choose always make sure the room is darkened so that you don't scare your hamster away.

If you believe your hamster could be in different rooms then put a bucket trap in each.

In daylight hours your Roborovski will probably be sleeping in whatever hiding place they've found so it will probably be evening time when they do creep out. You may want to stay up all night until they come home but if this isn't possible another way to find them would be to leave a couple of piles of treats in the room that they are in and sprinkle flour around each of them. If you count out a set number, for instance, six sunflower seeds, you will know if your hamster has taken any. Look carefully in the flour for any footprints and follow the tracks until you reach their hidey hole.

Other owners have had luck with tying large pieces of food such as whole peanuts in the shell to some string or yarn and leaving it out where your hamster can reach it. The hamster will gather it up and take it back to its new hiding place; all you have to do is follow the strands of yarn.
If you are using food remember to use one that will have a strong smell to your hamster in order for them to get the scent.

Remember your Roborovski Hamster won't think that it's lost or has made a great escape from prison. It has merely gone on a foraging adventure, much like its wild ancestors would. Therefore many do return to their cage so it is always a good idea to leave the cage door open (assuming of course there are no other hamsters in there), leave a trail of food leading up to the door and leave them. Sometimes they find their way home by themselves; after all they're bound to get hungry and thirsty eventually.

Another way of finding them is to turn off all the lights and sit quietly, listening for any scratching or chewing sounds. Some people recommend putting food on the floor and setting tin foil or crinkly cellophane on the floor near any possible hideouts, in doorways, near the cage and around the food. When your hamster creeps out you should hear them running about on the noisy paper.

If you have trained your hamster by talking to them then this is where that comes in handy as they will be used to the sound of your voice and scent they may come back if you call them quietly. I would always recommend that if your hamster lives in a family setting then the main care giver and handler searches for them as they will be more comfortable around that person. Don't have the whole household tearing up the place as this can be frightening for your hamster and there's more chance of your hamster getting injured.

Don't give up hope even if your hamster has been missing for hours. I've heard stories of hamsters that have been missing for days, even weeks and have been found with a stash of food under floorboards or in walls so listen carefully and look out for any small holes.

Once your hamster returns remember that they will most likely be tired. Don't try to play with them, instead calmly return them to their cage (assuming they didn't go back in themselves) ensure they have a fresh supply of food and water and leave them to rest.

Chapter 11: Hamster Clubs And Shows

Yes, there are actually Hamster Shows where you can take your hamster to be judged. I don't know how happy hamsters are about these shows, especially Roborovski Hamsters who aren't all that sociable with humans but I can see the appeal and I don't condemn anybody who wishes to take their hamster to a show and see how their pet measures up against others of the same breed.

Hamster Clubs

You don't actually need to be part of a Hamster Club in order to attend shows but there are advantages to doing so. Your membership fee covers a twelve month period regardless of when you join (as opposed to having to renew at the beginning of every year) so if you want to attend a couple of shows before joining a club you are able to do so.

In the UK there are three main regional clubs which are all affiliated with the National Hamster Council (NHC) who is the governing body. These clubs are the Southern Hamster Club (SHC) the Northern Hamster Club (NHC) and the Midland Hamster Club (MHC).

That's not to say there are no smaller clubs out there just that there are none that I know of that are associated with a regulatory body. There did used to be a British Hamster Association (BHA) who were affiliated with their own clubs and ran their own shows however this dissolved in 2007.

Why Join A Club?

All of the clubs and the National Hamster Council (NHC) are interested in promoting the welfare and responsible breeding of hamsters in the UK and on each website you can find information about the various types of hamsters, medical information and a list of breeders that are registered with the clubs.

By joining a club you may feel that you are part of a hamster community and you will be able to go to them for advice and help should you need to do so.

As well as having twelve months membership you will receive a hamster information sheet and a monthly journal which has up to date information on the shows that will be run that year.

Usually each club has around twelve shows a year which are held in a variety of places such as church halls, community centres, agricultural events and galas and it is far easier to have these sent directly to you via post or email rather than having to search the internet.

You can sometimes attend shows either for free or half price if you are a member of the club or some shows only allow you to enter the main show if you are part of the club. Pricing for each show is dependent upon the organiser (and may have changed between the time of writing and the time of publication) so always check beforehand.

Clubs sometimes host displays in order to inform the general public about the club and advise them about hamster related subjects such as different species, colours, coats and so on, again, being a member you should be informed of all of these events should you wish to attend.

How Much Does Membership Cost?
The clubs offer different membership options and cover adults, partnership (two or more people as members) junior (under 16 years of age), young adult (16-18 years of age) and family or school. The standard membership is £15 (around $20.29 US dollars) the paperless membership is the same as standard but as all the information such as show schedules and monthly journals are sent via email rather than the post it is cheaper at only £10 (around $13.53). Finally there is an affiliate membership which is £5 (around $6.76) and this is if you are already a member of one of the other clubs but want to join another region as well, for example, if you are part of the Northern Hamster Club (NHC) but think you would like to go to some of the Midland Hamster Club (MHC) shows or be part of their club too.

The Southern Hamster Club (SHC) and Midland Hamster Club (MHC) membership is slightly more expensive at £16 for standard membership ($21.64 US dollars) and £5.50 ($7.44 US dollars) Paperless membership costs the same but they are also open to international members. European membership costs £25 (around $33.81 US dollars) and rest of the world membership is £33 (around $44.63 US dollars)

You do appear to get a bit more with the Southern Hamster Club which could account for their extra fees. As well as the show schedules and a journal written by members each month including up to date hamster news, articles, letters and anything else the hamster enthusiast needs to know, their website also states that membership gives you access to advice on any topic of hamster care directly from an experienced exhibitor, judge or breeder, the opportunity to exhibit your hamster with the chance to win a trophy or rosette at their shows, access to the Member's Only Facebook

Group so you can chat to other members between shows and the National Hamster Council (NHC) handbook which contains the show standards and the guidelines that members must adhere to.

Payment is via the post using a cheque or postal order or online using PayPal or you can fill out your application form (printed from their website) and pay at one of the hamster shows.

Hamster Shows

Okay so you have a hamster settled happily in its new home and you decide that you want to enter it into a Hamster Show to see how well it measures up to others of its ilk. Where do you start?

You can start show life by becoming a club member and waiting for the show schedules to be sent to you but as mentioned above, you don't have to be a Hamster Club member in order to take part in the shows, you can just Google each club and look online at their show schedule and contact them to enter. My understanding is that the main show is usually for club members but the general public are able to enter Pet Classes for a fee (usually £1 which equates to around $1.35 in the US) but this is dependent upon the club and the organisers of each show so it is always worth clarifying whether you can participate in the main show.

Why Enter?

These types of shows are free for anyone to look around so I think if you are interested it is always worth going to see what it's all about regardless of whether you are participating or not.

Some people may frown upon these types of shows but I think that if you have a huge interest in these animals then these events are great to see other hamster breeds and meet experienced breeders and other hobbyists and owners.

It's a chance for you to talk about hamsters and share stories, anecdotes and care tips and discuss habitats. You may even make some new friends.

The judges' talks will give you an insight into the different species of hamsters so you may even learn a thing or two as well.

Sometimes hamster merchandise is available or you may even be able to reserve baby hamsters too.

What To Expect

Usually the club will state somewhere that the shows are judged to the National Hamster Council standards. These standards can be found on the National Hamster Council website or any of the individual club websites but you should also receive them in the handbook if you are a club member.

It is worth reading these standards before entering your pet into a show so that you know what they are being judged against.

Different clubs may have different rules but in the UK the various clubs are all pretty similar if not identical with regards to rules and guidelines.

Roborovski Hamsters were standardised in the UK in Two Thousand and Nine so your hamster must meet the show standards in order to place in the competition.
Your hamster will be judged against others of its species which means you won't have your Roborovski Hamster pitted against a Syrian Hamster and there are various categories they will earn points for.

These are type (25 points), fur (20 points) colour (30 points), size and condition (10 points each) and eyes and ears (5 points).

The ones with the best scores are the ones who place and win the competition.

In order to compete your hamster has to be healthy; taking a hamster that is sick could risk the health of the other hamsters in the competition and could lead to you being disqualified.

It should also be tame as the judges need to be able to lift the hamsters out of their cage in order to examine them and award them points so if your hamster refuses to be picked up at all then it is not worth taking them to a show.

Don't be put off by the thought of your hamster competing against 'award winning' high standard hamsters, with these type of shows it really is a case of the best on the day will win and they are more fun rather than serious and competitive like some pet shows.

How To Enter

The main show requires you to register your pet before the event so you will need to refer to the schedule in advance. This is where joining a club is beneficial as you should be sent all the show schedules in advance so you are less likely to miss them. However you can Google them and find the schedules that way.

Somewhere on the schedule will be the name and contact details of the Show Secretary as well as the date by which you have to register your pet.

You will need to know the species, coat type and colour as well as the class number for the hamster (on the show schedule you will find each species in a different class so you will need to check which one is for Roborovski Hamsters specifically) If you are showing more than one hamster then you will need the class number for each. You will also have to tell them which show you are entering – whilst different events have different Show Secretaries some will be the same for multiple shows. The last thing to tell them is whether you require a show pen. You can take your hamster in your own show pen but you will need to ensure it meets the required standards in both measurement and look. Most shows allow you to hire one for £1 but sometimes numbers are limited.

If you are unsure about any of these details then contact the Show Secretary and ask them. Just be aware that it may not be the same one for every show so make sure you are contacting the right person. Usually the organisers and people who attend these events are really helpful so don't be afraid to ask.

Most Show Secretaries will acknowledge that your entry has been received so that you know you are able to take part.

Usually entries are accepted via email although some may give a postal address or a telephone number as an alternative way of contacting.

Show Pens
All animals are judged anonymously therefore they must be put in approved show pens. These pens also allow the judges to easily lift out each hamster when required. As mentioned above they can be hired for £1 or you can buy your own.

The show pens must only contain approved items. This is substrate which for Roborovski Hamsters is usually wood shavings (which you have to bring yourself) a source of moisture which is usually a piece of vegetable because water bottles cannot be fixed to the Show pens, and approved food which is usually a dog biscuit that is provided by the show organisers. No other items are allowed in the cage so don't take any toys or tunnels or anything of that nature.

On The Day

It can look confusing when you enter a community centre or church hall or whatever the venue is and find lots of people rushing around or gathered in groups talking to each other. The best thing to do is to find the Show Secretary who will advise you what to do and will give you a show pen if you hired one in advance. To identify the Show Secretary look for someone who is sat at a table, surrounded by paperwork, they are often in a prominent place such as by the entrance or on the stage.

Most shows will have a table with show pen labels as well as dog biscuits for you to collect yourself so keep an eye out for this too or you may be directed to it when you collect your show pen.

The next thing to do is to put the correct substrate in the show pen, place the piece of vegetable that you are providing as a moisture source and dog biscuit inside.

Check your Roborovski Hamster over and then settle them in their cage.

Attach the pen label to the top left of the show pen and then take it over to the bench which is usually a long table used for judging, again the Show Secretary should direct you as to where and when to put your hamster down (also referred to as 'benching').

If unsure what to do always ask someone as club members are usually friendly and happy to help newcomers.

If you are early you may be able to put your hamster anywhere on the bench but if you arrive near enough on time you may see a Pen Steward organising the cages in which case you should ask them where they want you to place your show pen.

Before you leave your hamster make a note of your show pen number so that you can find the correct hamster later.

Judging

Once your hamster has been benched you can no longer have any contact with them or identify them as yours in any way within reach of the judges' hearing. To do so can get you disqualified as the judging needs to remain anonymous until the very end when the Show Secretary announces that they can be removed.

This is your opportunity to go and get a drink, have a look around and speak to other people. These shows usually attract experienced breeders and exhibitors so feel free to ask them for advice and tips if they're not busy. A good opening line is to ask if they have hamsters in the main show and what breed they have. If you don't want to speak to anybody then you are allowed to leave and return later just make sure you don't miss the end of the show!

The hamsters will be looked at in turn by a qualified judge who will remove each one from their cage and examine them, awarding points based on the attributes listed above. Usually they are helped by a Book Steward who will write down the judge's comments and add up the points.

The Pen Stewards will assist by placing the pens on the table and removing once the hamster has been judged.

Afterwards there may be a delay whilst the Show Secretary confirms that all the paperwork is correct and, once this task has been completed, they will announce that the hamsters can now be lifted from the bench. This is your cue to find your hamster and find out whether it has been placed.

You may find that the show pens are now in a different order as they will usually have been sorted according to the points they have been awarded with the highest scoring at one end and the lowest scoring at the other which is why it is important to take note of your show pen number in order to identify which hamster is yours.

Once collected, settle your hamster back in its carrier then clean out the show pen. You will need to return it in as good a condition as you took it in so make sure you clear out all the substrate and give it a wipe down, usually cage cleaning wipes of a cleaning spray will suffice.

Prizes
If your hamster has a coloured spot on its pen label then it has been placed in their category. A red spot means first place, blue spot is second place, and yellow and green are third and fourth place respectively.

If your hamster has been entered into a duplicate class then these aren't indicated on the show pen labels so you will need to check the show table to see if there are any prize cards with your name on it.

Rosettes will be given for every first placing hamster so it is worth hanging around for the presentation at the end if you have a red spot.

Pet Classes

As I mentioned before, members of the public are welcome to turn up on the day and enter the general pet classes. You can often even bring other small animals such as rabbits, guinea pigs, gerbils and so on. Entry is usually about £1 per animal.

Pet Classes are a good way to be introduced to a show as you don't have to decide whether to go in advance and you don't have to stay all day.

They usually have fun categories and games too such as 'fastest in a hamster ball' or 'hamster bowling'.

American Hamster Clubs And Shows

As far as I'm aware there is only one hamster club in America which is the California Hamster Club who host shows throughout the year. As with the UK clubs their rules and guidelines are online as is their show calendar.

Entry fees for the shows are $1 for members and $2 for none members whilst the fun/pet classes are a block fee meaning you pay one price and are automatically entered into all of the pet and fun classes on that day. Entry for those are $2.50 for members and $4 for none members.

Again, as with the UK shows there are guidelines as to what type of bedding and show pen is needed.

Chapter 12: Breeding

I have already mentioned that hamsters are prolific breeders and you run the risk of buying one that is already pregnant, especially from pet shops as due to their genitalia being so tiny it is hard to differentiate between the genders unless you are an absolute expert. However breeding Roborovski Hamsters to sell isn't as easy as just putting them into a cage and leaving them alone for a few days.

Why Are You Breeding?

This is the question that should be answered honestly *before* you breed. If the answer is "to make money" then I would strongly dissuade you from breeding at all because it is not the money spinner you may think it is. Firstly pet shops already have their own breeders established and are unlikely to buy from anyone else, especially someone who may have just started breeding recently. Secondly, for the reason mentioned above, there are far too many unwanted litters out there which end up in animal shelters (if they're lucky). Thirdly breeding and looking after the babies then finding forever homes can take time as well as space and money; you are going to need large cages in which to separate your babies once they are a few weeks' old as well as extra feeding dishes, water bottles and toys, not to mention the extra food.

If your reason to breed is because you want baby Roborovski Hamsters I would strongly suggest you contact a few animal shelters and ask them to notify you when they have any babies taken in or keep checking the 'Preloved' websites on the internet to see if anybody is selling. Breeding your own just because you want one or two new baby hamsters isn't the most sensible idea – what happens if your female has a litter of eight, would you be able to take proper care of all of them forever?

If your reason for breeding is because you love these animals and it is an extension of your hobby I can understand this. I would never encourage anybody to breed but the best people to do so are those who are truly love these animals, have been caring for them for a long time and have the space, money and time to care for them properly without being in a rush to sell them off to just anybody.

Regardless of your reasons why, if you do breed your animals I would always recommend you try and find homes for them *beforehand* as this way you are not going to find yourself with an unwanted litter to take care of and panic about how you are going to afford to keep them. Ask friends and family as well as any contacts in the hamster community you may have, for example, via forums, social media sites, through any hamster club you may be a member of or at shows. Sometimes other breeders will take them from you in order to renew the bloodlines of the animals they breed and avoid inbreeding.

When To Breed
Roborovski Hamsters reach sexual maturity at six to eight weeks of age and whilst in the wild they may mate at a very young age it is not recommended that you breed domesticated ones so early and they should be separated by gender until they are older. The absolute minimum age is four months but ideally the female should be around five to seven months in order to be fully grown and mature and strong enough to raise a litter.

Usually Roborovski Hamsters will only breed in the Spring and Summer months when the weather is warmer and the female usually won't have her first litter until the Spring after she was born. It is thought that this is because either the males become temporarily sterile or the females don't come into season due to the colder temperatures. However as light and temperature clearly plays a part in mating habits and fertility, theoretically, hamsters kept as pets could breed all year round which is something that needs to be considered when putting two hamsters of the opposite sex together.

Considerations Before Breeding
Yes you could put two Roborovski Hamsters of the opposite sex in a cage together and hope nature takes its course but if you want to be a responsible breeder and create the best animals you possibly can then you need to think carefully about which hamsters you are breeding.

Just putting two creatures together simply because you have a male and a female can result in babies that have birth defects, OCD, Spinning, brain damage and other conditions. To produce the best pets you really need to know what you are doing so I would advise you speak to experienced breeders first and ask for as much advice as you possibly can.

If you are breeding then you want to pair up hamsters that have the best chance of giving birth to healthy offspring with calm and friendly temperaments as these are easier to tame and generally make better pets. You should also consider trying to breed hamsters that meet the National Hamster Council requirements as this may give you a better chance of selling them although it isn't always guaranteed that every hamster born will be of show standard.

Think of selecting two hamsters to breed as being a bit like choosing a Pedigree dog. Don't just pick two hamsters that look good; only purchase from reputable and experienced breeders who have kept thorough records on the animals they have bred. You should know the history of both hamsters and ideally their family tree should go back at least three generations. If possible try to see the parents' of the hamsters you are choosing in order to see what features they have and how they behave as this will give you an idea of what their offspring will be like.

DO NOT breed any hamsters you have purchased from an animal shelter or from a previous owner because you will not know enough about their family history and could end up with offspring that have birth defects.

Roborovski Hamsters can be quite picky and potential mates should be fully compatible with each other as those that live and play harmoniously together will produce better babies than those that don't. Each pair is different and some breeders report that they have sometimes paired up two Roborovski Hamsters that have immediately bred whilst others have lived together for a very long time before mating. Sometimes pairs have stayed together for life, seemingly happy together yet have never produced any babies.

Once you have chosen two unrelated hamsters and they are old enough to start breeding make sure you take them to a vet to ensure they are one hundred percent healthy and fit enough to rear a litter of pups.

Your hamsters should both be in the best condition possible before placing them in the same cage – think of them as mini athletes training for the Olympics. They should have a healthy diet and be fed extra protein, vitamins and minerals. This can be given in the form of well cooked egg either hard boiled or scrambled, plain cooked chicken or fresh fruit – all of which should be cut up very small and given in small portions, one or two small pieces should suffice. If you want to vary their diet you can also give them diced tofu, plain yoghurt and low fat cottage cheese, again, tiny portions only.

Many breeders recommend sprinkling Brewer's Yeast Powder on their food as well.

This high quality food regime should be continued once they have been paired up, during pregnancy, birth and whilst the litter is being raised.

The mother will need extra nutrients in order to ensure that she produces enough milk to feed the babies. If not she may become stressed and start to eat her young. (See Section Below – Cannibalism)

Introducing

Clean out a cage beforehand with some pet safe disinfectant. You can use a diluted bleach and warm water solution as long as you ensure that any traces of this has been thoroughly washed away before putting in your hamsters. The purpose of cleaning is to remove the scent of any other hamster that may have lived in the cage, even if it is the male or female that you are breeding; the cage needs to be neutral territory. All toys and accessories that you may eventually place in the cage also need to be clean and free of animal scents too.

Once clean put in a deep layer of wood shavings or whatever substrate you use and spread it out so the entire floor is covered. Roborovski Hamsters can become territorial over food dishes so simply spread out two or three handfuls of food around the cage rather than using a dish or a bowl.

Next put in two water bottles so the hamsters can have one each. You can use a bowl but it is not recommended as they tend to splash about and wet the substrate and bedding which can be uncomfortable for the hamsters and also because babies can easily drown in a water bowl as they wander around the cage, remember they are blind at birth. If you do use water bowls remember to change them for water bottles before the babies are born.

Finally add some nesting material and your cage will be ready for the hamsters.

Some people will say put in the male first but you can put them in at the same time and this has the advantage that neither of them have any dominance so are all on even footing.

Keep a close eye on them for any signs of fighting. The hamsters will sniff, chase, squeak (a lot!) and may even 'box' but these are all normal behaviours and they will eventually settle down within a couple of days. If blood is drawn or there is a visible wound or cut or either hamster appears stressed then separate the pair immediately and repeat again at a later date if you wish to try again.

Once the squeaking and boxing has stopped you can start to add toys and wheels to the cage. It is important to add two of each type of toy as well as two wheels to reduce any arguments that may occur. It would be wise to

81

introduce just one type of toy every couple of days and monitor so that if it causes fighting you can remove it immediately.

You may see the hamsters 'mount' each other but this doesn't actually mean that copulation is taking place, sometimes this is just to establish dominance and you may even find hamsters of the same sex doing this to each other.

Before Birth

It is important that you clean the cage *before* the babies are born, once they have arrived you will need to leave the cage and hamster family alone. Also you should remove the hamster wheels as there is a risk that the female could give birth whilst running or the parents' may take the babies to the wheel which is dangerous.

You will see the hamsters start to make a nest and whilst it is not always necessary to provide them with a house to use as a family nest you may wish to do this as sometimes when the wheels have been removed Roborovski Hamsters have a tendency to start running laps of the cage and they run the risk of trampling the nest and babies whilst doing so.

A problem with trying to clean the cage and remove the wheels and water bowls before the birth is that your female Roborovski Hamster will put on very little (if any) weight and won't usually show that she is pregnant until nearing the end of her pregnancy, usually around day seventeen or eighteen and this is usually only if she is having a large litter so unless you actually see mating take place you won't really know that she is expecting therefore if you know you are breeding I would recommend you clean the cage on a regular basis (every couple of weeks) just to ensure that this has been done. If you really need to you can remove the wheel after the babies have been born as long as you are quick and disturb the hamsters as little as possible.

The Babies

If you don't happen to see your female give birth you will know as soon as the babies have been born because they will make a lot of noise which could be described as chirping. The bigger the babies get, the noisier they will be especially when food is brought back to the nest.

Remember to continue to give the extra protein and vitamins in their diet but increase the amount of food you give when the babies are over a week old as this is when food will be taken back to the nest for them.

The babies will be pink and furless and their eyes will be firmly closed when born. At around twelve to fourteen days their eyes will begin to open but they may blindly wander around the cage a few days before this. Don't worry if you see one wander away, one of the parents will bring it back to the nest eventually.

At this stage you should leave your hamster family alone. Only go near the cage to give water and food and these tasks should be done as quickly and as quietly as possible. However tempting it may be DO NOT touch the babies or the parents.

Once the young are spending more time away from the nest you should be able to clean out the cage but make sure this is done quickly so as not to cause too much stress for the parents. Keep some of the old nest so that you can put back in otherwise the parents will feel lost as the cage won't smell the same.

By three weeks the babies should be handled as much as possible in order to become tame and friendly towards humans. It may take a few days or weeks for them to stop wriggling and allow you to hold them but it is worth the time and patience as they will make better pets if they are tame. Be prepared for them to be very jumpy. Always sit down and hold them either close to the floor or over a large box with a good layer of substrate/nesting material to cushion their fall.

After three weeks the babies can be removed from their parents and put in new cages. Ideally they should be kept together in order to get used to being without their mother but should be separated by gender by twenty eight days.

Give the babies as much food as they can eat, including the food with the extra protein and vitamins and minerals. Each hamster should have a wheel of its own and there should be lots of tubes, toys, hiding places and so on to reduce arguments and keep them stimulated.

You should give them each a health check on a daily basis.

Roborovski Fathers
You may notice that the male Roborovski Hamster is very attentive during the pregnancy and birth; he will help to build the nest, take food back for the mother and babies and will help to raise the litter. He will even put up with the females' bad moods and you may see him sulking in a corner somewhere in the cage when she has banished him from the nest.

Whilst you may coo over how kind and loving he is, remember he has an ulterior motive and this is that the female is fertile again as soon as she's given birth and the male will want to mate again. If this happens then another litter could be born twenty one days later.

Subsequent Litters

Being pregnant and rearing another litter back to back is not healthy for the female. Some will deal with it better than others and if your female doesn't look too thin or too tired and appears to be a good mother to her babies then you may not mind if she has another litter so close to the first in which case you may be happy to leave the male in the cage to help her rear the litter and allow nature to take its course. It is not recommended that you do this indefinitely however and if your female does have a second litter straight after the first then you must remove the male after the babies have been born as a third litter could be far too much for your female (and you) to cope with.

Whilst it is possible for a female Roborovski to simultaneously rear two litters I would worry about the babies getting enough milk especially in the first few hours as first milk is incredibly important to newborns and I would recommend that you actually remove the first litter.

Once they reach twenty one days the hamster babies should be weaned and can live without their parents but timing is very important when removing them. If you do this too early it can be stressful for the mother who may wander the cage searching for her babies. Removing the first litter either as she gives birth or just after means that she won't miss them as she will have the new litter to occupy her attention however as you shouldn't really disturb the mother after she has given birth it is better to try and remove the first litter a day or two before she is due to give birth. A tip a breeder once gave me was to remove all but one just before she has the new litter. The remaining baby will keep her company and then once she gives birth to the new litter it is far easier to catch and remove the remaining baby rather than trying to catch a whole litter.

Re-homing

As mentioned above the hamsters can theoretically leave their parents after three weeks once they are weaned – always make sure that each hamster is eating by itself before you take them away from their mother.

It is far better to keep the hamsters a little longer is possible, ideally until at least seven weeks before sending them off to new homes. This enables you to ensure they are healthy and there are no underlying medical conditions apparent. By this age they will also be tamer and friendlier towards humans.

Hopefully you will have found suitable homes for the hamsters before they were even born (or at least have started looking after your female gave birth) so by seven weeks you should be able to simply allow their new owners to collect them.

If you cannot find homes yourself for your hamsters and you cannot keep them indefinitely then you may consider sending them to an animal shelter but this really should be a last resort. If you can advertise them yourself via forums or internet sites that specialise in people selling hamsters.

One thing I will say is please don't be in a hurry to re-home your baby hamsters and *never* sell them as Pinkies. Pinkies is the term that is given to newborn hamsters because they have no fur. Not only is it incredibly stressful and cruel for the mother to have her babies removed so early but the babies will most likely be used as reptile food. No matter what anybody tells you they cannot be successfully weaned and raised from such a young age.

Colonies
Roborovski Hamsters can be bred in colonies but it is far more difficult than breeding pairs and should only be done by an expert who has had many years raising and breeding these creatures.

If you keep more than one male in a colony you may find that they fight over the females and you may find that squabbles break out between the females.

Another problem is that although a colony will raise babies together you may find that one female tries to steal another hamster's babies.

Remember the more hamsters you have the more space you will need, the more introductions you will need to make, the more toys, wheels and water bottles are needed and the more chances there are for fighting. Each hamster should be checked regularly to make sure there are no wounds or bullying and that neither of them are prevented from eating or drinking.

Males need to be unrelated to the females but as the females could all have babies it will be impossible to identify which babies belong to which female if they are all born around a similar time. This means that if there are any genetic problems with any of the babies you won't know which female to stop breeding from. Ideally the females will sisters or if this isn't possible then at least from the same bloodline in order to minimize the chances of their being any genetic defects.

Cannibalism

Sadly some Roborovski Hamsters do eat their young but the chances of this can be minimized if you know the reasons for it.

Males may eat their offspring if he sees them as a threat to mating with the female which is why it may be a good idea to separate him once you know your female is pregnant or just after.

Females will eat their young for a variety of reasons, mainly if she perceives a threat to the nest or her babies. These include;

Predatory animals – keep all other pets such as cats, dogs and so on in a separate room from your hamsters. If you are breeding it is wise to give your hamsters a room to themselves, away from any other creatures that could be seen as a threat.

Human Scent – Don't ever pick up or touch a baby until they are old enough to be separated and you know that they are fully weaned otherwise the mother could reject her babies or more likely, eat them should she catch even the slightest whiff of your scent on them.

Overcrowding – Make sure the cage is big enough for all your hamsters, even if you are breeding a pair rather than a colony you should always have the biggest cage you possibly can.

Lack Of Food – Always provide plenty of food for every hamster otherwise the mother may eat them so that they don't starve to death.

Lack Of Protein – Continue to give the mother (and the rest of the hamsters) a diet that is high in protein because if she lacks this she will eat her young as a way of gaining protein.

Too Young – Another reason not to breed your hamsters younger than five months is that if they are no mature enough to cope with a litter they may eat them just to get rid of them. Sometimes a young mother may deem her own babies to be a threat to her.

Illness – If the mother senses that one or more of her babies is sick or has a birth defect, rather than let them suffer she will eat them.

Other reasons include too few babies, inability to produce enough milk for them all or too many babies to feed.

Remember if a mother eats her baby it isn't because she hates them or is intentionally killing them out of cruelty but because of another underlying issue. In her mind she is being kind because eating them will be seen as a humane way of killing them rather than allowing them to suffer from whatever perceived illness or threat she has sensed.

The best way to prevent cannibalism is to separate the male and female as soon as she falls pregnant or immediately after the babies are born, feed a protein rich diet and prove plenty of food and water. Keep them in a spacious cage in a quiet room and try not to disturb them.

Breeding Facts
The female will be fertile every four days which means there are plenty of opportunities for your hamster to become pregnant.

Gestation period (length of pregnancy) is around twenty to twenty two days although some have been as long as thirty days.

A Roborovski female can have between one and eight babies in a litter although four to six is the norm.

Roborovski Hamsters may have a break between litters after a few litters have been born in succession.

They may not mate in winter months although higher temperatures and artificial lighting which can make the length of daytime feel longer may mean that hamsters procreate all year round.

Males are fertile their whole life but females usually become sterile around two years of age.

Pups are born blind and without fur. They are totally dependent upon their mothers who will nurse them, clean them and keep them warm.

Questions Asked

Can A Roborovski Hamster Be Microchipped?

Microchipping pets is all the rage at the moment and whilst I think it's great for cats and dogs that may go missing away from home unfortunately it's not an option for Roborovski Hamsters.

Firstly they are far too small to endure having a chip inserted into their body and I fear the stress of the needle would have an adverse effect on them.

Secondly there isn't much point in microchipping; Roborovski Hamsters should really be kept indoors so if they escape they are most likely going to be in the house. Sadly I don't feel that a Roborovski Hamster that found its way outside would survive long enough to be found and if it did being captured by a total stranger would be nigh on impossible. Even on the off chance that anyone saw it (remember these are incredibly fast creatures adept at burrowing and hiding) I doubt they would think to catch it and take it to the vet as they would probably see it as a rodent rather than a beloved pet that could be microchipped.

The best way to keep your pet safe is to ensure it is in it a locked cage at all times and is constantly supervised whenever it is taken out. I would always make sure it is still in some type of enclosure such as a large cardboard box so that it can't wander too far when away from its cage.

Can hamsters eat grass?

The answer is yes, hamsters can eat grass and they would out in the wild but nowadays there are lots of harmful substances that can be on the grass in our gardens or surrounding fields. Pesticides, plant food and other animals' urine can all make your pet hamster ill. Too much can also give your pet an upset stomach. I would always recommend giving other foods to your hamster rather than grass but if you do give it then wash it thoroughly.

Should My Hamster's Cage Be Heated?

A normal room temperature of 18-26 degrees Celsius (65-80 degrees Fahrenheit) is fine for your Roborovski. Make sure that their enclosure isn't in direct sunlight or in a draughty area so try to keep them away from windows.

Many people will worry about their hamster's temperature and can over compensate by overheating the room. My tip would be that if you are too hot or too cold then your hamster will probably be too. Remember if they are cold then they can burrow into their bedding so always provide a material that will keep enable them to keep warm.

Whilst they can tolerate a bit more heat or a slightly lower temperature, 15 degrees Celsius (60 degrees Fahrenheit) or lower can cause your hamster to quickly become ill so it is always a good idea to check the temperature in your pet's room on a regular basis.

Can I Give My Hamster A Bath?

The short answer is no! Don't ever bath a Roborovski Hamster in water. Not only does it stress them out but it removes the natural essential oils form their fur which can lead to health problems. They can also catch a cold which can be fatal for these creatures. They will spend twenty percent of their time grooming themselves so water is not necessary but if you are worried that they are unclean then provide a sand bath. Unfortunately some hamsters do have a strong smell but this is natural and you will never get rid of it.

I have seen forums where people have said that if a hamster has something toxic on their fur then you can bathe them in warm water, use baby shampoo and dry with a towel but even this can cause them to become ill and it will be incredibly stressful. Please ignore the advice that says you can dry your Roborovski with a hairdryer as not only can it lead to accidental burns but it will increase their stress levels so astronomically it could kill them.

Their cage should always be free of toxic and sticky materials but if they did accidentally escape and/or get into something they shouldn't and you were worried about them being poisoned then you should cut the offending item out very carefully with nail scissors or wipe them down with the corner of a warm, damp washcloth then immediately use a paper towel or dry cloth to absorb the moisture. Again both of these should only be done as a very last resort only and this is a case of prevention being better than cure so keep your hamster safe in its cage away from any materials that are likely to cause them harm.

Do Hamsters Bite?

Some hamsters do bite humans whenever they are picked up but the Roborovski Hamster isn't one of them. They are so timid they would rather run away and hide than stay and fight. If cornered they may indeed give a sharp nip but this is very rare from these small creatures and they would have to be very frightened. If you are worried about your hamster biting then you could wear gloves when handling but the best way to deal with biting is to be as calm as possible when handling and never grab or startle your hamster if you can help it. Whilst a sharp nip does hurt, try not to shake your hamster off as this can cause them injury.

Conclusion

Roborovski Hamsters make amazing pets and are super fun to watch however as they can become stressed very easily it is important that they are kept in quiet homes away from other animals and should only be cared for by older children under adult supervision. Young children should not really handle these type of hamsters as they can be loud, rough and over excitable which can frighten these timid creatures.

Although they can be tamed they are far happier to live their lives in their own enclosures but an owner can get enjoyment just by providing lots of toys and observing their antics.

If keeping more than one Roborovski in a cage make sure the enclosure is big enough and keep a close eye on them in case any arguments break out. Remember two of everything is an absolute must, like toddlers, these creatures don't really like to share!

A Roborovski Hamster can be bought fairly cheaply although you may have to do some research and wait awhile if you want one that is up to Hamster Show standard. Some people may balk at paying nearly ten times as much for the cage as they paid for the hamster but I would always recommend anyone who is going to own one of these invests in a high quality cage that provides plenty of space for the hamster to run around. Monthly costs can be kept low if you are careful to re-use bedding that isn't soiled, don't waste food by overfeeding and make your own toys.

An absolute must have is a hamster wheel in order for these creatures to get the exercise they need to stay healthy and happy. A wide variety of toys will keep them occupied and again, are incredibly important in order to keep prevent them becoming bored. Boredom leads to OCD behaviours or can encourage them to try and escape their cages.

Finally please remember to never breed unless you have absolute certainty that the litter that is born is going to be wanted and if possible, find homes for the babies before you breed. Whilst it may be a fun hobby, there is not a high demand for these creatures and you will only be adding to the high number of unwanted babies already out there.

11166892R00051

Printed in Great Britain
by Amazon